MOTHERS *of* MOLESTATION SURVIVORS

Mothers of Molestation Survivors:
Supporting Moms to Make a Difference in Their Children's Lives
First Edition Copyright ©2011 by Kim D. Johnson, L.C.S.W.
Second Edition Copyright ©2012 by Kim D. Johnson, L.C.S.W.
Third Edition Copyright © 2023 by Kim D. Johnson, L.C.S.W.

Published in the United States of America

ISBN   Paperback: 978-1-960629-33-3
ISBN   eBook: 978-1-960629-34-0

Disclaimer:

The stories and names in this book have been changed to protect the mothers, children, siblings, and even the perpetrators. The names, circumstances, and details have been altered carefully to protect those involved while allowing the stories still to make significant and valid points.

Please address all inquiries to:
Kim D. Johnson, L.C.S.W. 916-780-2575
helpmoms@yahoo.com
www.transformyourlifecounseling.com

Edited by: Tyler Tichelaar
Cover Design & Interior Layout: Ericka Obando & Daniel Lopez
For more information please visit: www.transformyourlifecounseling.com

ReadersMagnet, LLC
10620 Treena Street, Suite 230 | San Diego, California, 92131 USA
1.619. 354. 2643 | www.readersmagnet.com

MOTHERS *of* MOLESTATION SURVIVORS

KIM D. JOHNSON

ReadersMagnet, LLC

Table of Contents

KIM JOHNSON &

MOTHERS OF MOLESTATION SURVIVORS

"Kim's insight not only liberated my daughter from a life of internalized torment, but she gave me the courage with honesty to overcome my own fears. Kim showed us we could speak out, we could overcome social destruction, and we could be radiant and strong in the absolute truth. Kim's work lives on and on and on as my grown daughter and I have intimate conversations with women in surprising places of everyday life. We listen, witness, and tell our story of a restored life after molestation because of the steadfast help we received from Kim. Her book is a gift and tool of inspiration for recovery. Thank you, Kim, for holding out the brightly lit candle of life restored and showing us a path of power and hope."

— Lisa Pierini

"As a sexual abuse survivor myself, I am keenly sensitive to and aware of the need for community awareness and training in regard to the healing of those who been sexually violated. I am extremely proud of the work Kim Johnson continues to do with sexual abuse survivors, and for her passion to educate the mothers who are drawn into the victimization cycle as well.

I found Kim's book to be extremely informative and deeply insightful in her approach to educating and supporting the moms of those children who have been abused. Not only will it provide a platform of encouragement and empowerment to the mothers who are so often disregarded, but it will most assuredly, and finally, gives them a voice."

— Rev. Rhonda Perryman

"Kim Johnson has touched my life in a very meaningful way. Throughout our therapeutic relationship, she has helped me find an inner peace and an integration of all the very different conflicting parts of myself that dealt with my child abuse in a myriad of ways. Presently, thanks to our work together, I feel safe, secure, peaceful, and have found a love for me that I once thought would never come to be. Thank you for writing such an important work, Kim!"

— Samantha, Sacramento, California

"Kim Johnson's gift of hearing and loving hearts into wholeness permeates the very essence of this book. Her compassionate, research-based insight and clinical experience has birthed a ground-breaking work that will facilitate the healing of child sexual abuse survivors by supporting the mothers who love, care for, and protect them. Whether you have a child or not, read this book. Chances are someone you know could benefit from the enlightened understanding that you will be able to offer them as a result."

— Judy Williamson, Sacramento CA

"What a breath of fresh air! I was so inspired by this resourceful book and Kim's passion to help MOMS find a voice and a safe haven for support. As the aunt of a child who was hurt, I was hurt. I felt somewhat helpless, and I didn't know what we should do next. I, now, am so inspired to be the Educated, Resourceful, and Spiritual Mother who can protect my own two young girls and be a loud voice to bring awareness and help to others! Unfortunately, this problem will not go away, but we can change how many victims it will touch. God Bless Kim, and those who serve to make a difference for a MOM or child! Pain is weakness leaving the body. We all will go through painful experiences, but we can work through them, and they are not in vain. We can move into a new place with new hope and be strong again."

— J. Marsh, Roseville, CA

ENDORSEMENTS FROM FELLOW AUTHORS AND EXPERTS IN SOCIAL WORK AND CHILD SEXUAL ABUSE ISSUES:

"Kim Johnson has created a most valuable guide for mothers who have experienced the trauma of their child being sexually molested. In her book Mothers of Molestation Survivors, Johnson uses real-life stories to create a tapestry ranging from listing symptoms of sexual abuse to how to respond with compassion. Johnson writes, 'When a child reveals to her mother she has been hurt in a sexual manner, how a mother responds establishes a path of recovery for the child.' Having worked with hundreds of adults who have been sexually abused as children, I believe this book with all its factual information will inform, comfort, and help heal many lives."

— Barbara Sinor, Ph.D., author of *Gifts From the Child Within*
and An Inspirational Guide for the Recovering Soul

"This book is going to be an amazing resource for the countless women I see who've experienced sexual abuse, as well as those who minister to them. It will also give these women back their voices to protect their own children, and empower them to break the cycle of abuse from generation to generation. Kim has done an incredible work, and on behalf of all those who will be the grateful recipients, myself included, Thank you!"

— Barbara Wilson, author of *The Invisible Bond: How to Break*
Free from Your Sexual Past

"A fantastic resource for children and families learning to survive and thrive after child molestation. Society needs more books addressing this very important issue so we can learn how to help not just the child but the family learns to move past such a terrible experience. Every resource center, professional, teacher and any others dealing with this subject needs a copy on their shelves.

— Chynna Laird, author of the award-winning memoir, *Not Just Spirited: A Mom's Sensational Journey With Sensory Processing Disorder (SPD)*

"Kim Johnson's book shines a light on a societal group that simply has not received the support or attention it deserves— the mothers of the molested. Johnson's years of experience provide unprecedented insight into the issue. This book is a must-read for those seeking to understand the 'battle' these mothers go through and for those willing and able to support them."

— Julie Phillips Randles, freelance journalist

"Finally, the voices of this most overlooked group of survivors of the trauma of sexual abuse—the mothers—are being heard. In this significant and long overdue book, Kim Johnson, LCSW, brings to light the courageous battles these women endure as they fight to protect their children, and themselves, from the ravages and denial of this destructive and all-too-common occurrence in the sanctity of their family members' lives."

— Nancy Bethem, L.C.S.W.

"When a child has been sexually abused, it is often the mother who becomes the most important person in the recovery. Kim Johnson provides a much-needed manual for mothers describing the necessary actions that must be taken for healing to occur. She also clearly, but compassionately, describes the struggles, pitfalls, and conflicts that can impede healing. I highly recommend this resource for any mom who finds that her child has been sexually or emotionally abused."

— Dean A. Dickerson, Ph.D., EMDRIA Certified Therapist and Approved Consultant, Board Certified Expert in Traumatic Stress, www.pratherapists.com

"The mother of a child traumatized by molestation experiences her own trauma of wrenching anguish and guilt, often with nowhere to turn. Her own recovery is both critical and courageous. This book offers the tools of recovery and spiritual healing. Bravo!"

— Laurie Peters, M.D. in Psychiatry

"Finally! Kim Johnson, LCSW provides a safe harbor for Mothers of Sexually Abused Children. She has a unique understanding of the tightrope these mothers walk. It is a great step forward in bringing this topic out of hiding and into a safe fellowship for healing and transformation for these children and their mothers."

— Susan A. Rold, MS, MFT

"Mothers of Molestation Survivors provide a revealing look into the world of child sexual abuse, and will give confidence to mothers to recognize sexual abuse, respond, and write about their circumstances."

—Jill Osborne EdS, LPC, author of *Sam Feels Better Now*

Mothers of Molestation Survivors

Supporting Moms to Make a Difference in Their Children's Lives

NEW YORK

Kim D. Johnson

LICENSED CLINICAL SOCIAL WORKER

To my supportive, loving husband, Dan: thank you for being so patient while I spent hours discussing, researching, writing, and promoting this book. It would have been so much harder to achieve my goal without your listening to my ideas, encouraging me to continue, and affirming my mission to reach Mothers of Molestation Survivors through these pages.

To my precious children, Gabriella and Garrett: when I look at you, I am reminded of why mothers need to be supported to protect and save their dear ones. Children are the most important part of who a mother is, and you two are no exception. Your beautiful eyes, hearts, and spirits encourage and inspire me.

Lastly, to all who have chosen to protect their children no matter what the cost. You are some of the most courageous, heroic women I have known. Your reward will come most certainly in eternity. This Bible verse says it all: "…the world was not worthy of them." — Hebrews 11:38 (New International Version)

ACKNOWLEDGEMENTS

I would like to express gratitude to the mothers who were willing to be interviewed. Your stories inspired me to write this book. You were very courageous in sharing in this endeavor.

My family members need to be acknowledged for their support during this ten-year process. Thank you to my brother, for without his humor, I couldn't have continued. I appreciate my sister for her candor and brilliant ideas. My mother has been there in some of my darkest moments and without her, I couldn't have survived. Thanks, Mom!

All we need are a handful of loyal and trustworthy friends; they are worth more than gold. I would like to acknowledge my invaluable friends Elizabeth Douglas and Rebecca Lucero. They have been consistent, compassionate, and strong as I have struggled personally and professionally.

I would like to thank the other therapists and professionals with whom I have collaborated and consulted. Their clinical input, suggestions, and wisdom have contributed to this book's content and substantiated the reality of the situations experienced by Mothers of Molestation Survivors.

BY

Marjorie McKinnon

The awareness of the subject of sexual child abuse has been on the rise. The public is finally starting to believe it actually happens. Sixty million survivors of sexual child abuse should not be ignored. One in four girls and one in six boys will be sexually abused at some time during their childhood. Ninety percent of the perpetrators will be known to the child. A lot of mothers are behind those children, and a large number of them have no idea what is happening to their loved ones.

I know, for I was a mother who had two daughters, ages four and five, who were sexually molested by my second husband. I didn't find out about it until I was halfway through recovery in my mid-forties. My youngest daughter, who was raped at gunpoint when she was seventeen, not knowing I had never known about his abuse, blurted it out. The shock dropped me to my knees. I called both girls and they explained, almost shame-faced, about the abuse they had endured, and how they had never told me because my husband was so busy beating me up in drunken rages and cheating on me that they didn't want to add to my problems.

How do you deal with the shame of not being there for those you love the most? How do you address and applaud their courage in the face of such danger, knowing it should have been you, not them?

And yet it was me, as it was so many of the mothers of these children. My father raped me at the age of thirteen, but I had never dealt with it until long after my children were grown. Being a survivor of sexual child abuse doesn't come near to the emotional pain that being the mother of one does. The shock of finding out your child is not only vulnerable but has already been targeted and abused almost makes you lose your mind with grief and helplessness. The guilt, the anger, the unbelievable horror that this can't possibly have happened to your child overwhelms you. I confronted this man on his death bed. He admitted to the abuse, but he said it was my daughters' fault. I was appalled that even at death's door he couldn't accept responsibility.

I have not read much on how these mothers can deal with what happens to their loved ones. There isn't much out there. But Kim Johnson's book, Mothers of Molestation Survivors (or MOMS as she calls them), hits you right between the eyes. She pulls no punches as she explains what happens not only to the child, but especially to the mother, and what she needs to do about it.

I read Kim Johnson's book the day after Mother's Day. I had no mother to congratulate, hug, or send flowers or a card to that day. My mother died when I was nineteen, but if she were alive today, she, along with my father, she would be in prison. Rage and helplessness resurrected in me as I read these pages and identified with so much of what was said. It was the first time I'd ever heard it set out in such a practical and yet compassionate manner for those of us who were survivors or had children who were victims (or maybe both). I felt the stabilizing hand of Ms. Johnson's wisdom as she breaks down four major areas: Understanding, Change, Healing, and Transformation. She explains the four different kinds of mothers who are dealt these cards: the Protective Mother, the Un-Protective Mother, the Over-Protective Mother, and the Co-Perpetrator Mother. She shows us why they do what they do and what kind of imprint it places on their children.

Ms. Johnson has great admiration for the Protective Mothers, fighting battles to protect their children, and she shares several stories of both mothers and children, illustrating the four kinds of mothers, what happened to them, and how they dealt with it. She summarizes and then gives exercises after each story— questions that probe your mind and unload bursts of anguish you didn't know were buried inside your troubled heart. You feel the healing begin.

She lists six beliefs that an educated mother of molested children must contend with in order to protect her child and bring change. She describes ways to heal and find peace.

Here is a book the world needs, a book that addresses the needs of a lost member of the human race, the mothers of molested children. We are all so busy trying to help the little ones that we forget about the ones who gave birth to them. And yet, children of an untreated sexual child abuse victim stand a five times greater chance of being abused. We must help the mothers if we are going to save the children.

So, MOMS of the world, get busy. Get this book and begin the healing journey that Ms. Johnson guides you through.

— Marjorie McKinnon Author of *REPAIR Your Life: A Program for Recovery from Incest and Childhood Sexual Abuse* Founder of www.thelamplighters.org, an international movement for Incest and Child Abuse Recovery

FIGHTING THE BATTLE
MAKING THE DIFFERENCE

In the media, we constantly hear about children who have been molested. We are aware of their trauma. But what trauma is experienced by their family members? Specifically, how does a mother cope with knowing her child has been molested? As a licensed clinical social worker who has often worked with molested children, I wanted to know what resources were available to mothers of molestation survivors (MOMS) and why we do not hear more about them. When I surveyed the public about this group of women, my guess was confirmed— most people have given little thought to what it would be like to be the mother of a molestation survivor. As I interviewed the MOMS themselves, I learned that few had shared their stories before.

I believe that mothers of molestation survivors are struggling but potentially inspiring women who deserve to have their stories told. More importantly, I believe their stories can help mothers of sexually abused children work through the process of healing by understanding how other mothers have coped with the situation—and hopefully prevent other children from being sexually abused. This book is written for all mothers of molested children, family members and friends who want to understand the situation better and offer support, and it is written for everyone who cares about protecting children from molestation. My goal is for you, the support family. We must support families and their children as they cope with the trauma they have experienced if we are to heal our communities.

My perspective on child molestation and how it affects mothers is colored by my thirty-year career in private practice as a licensed clinical social worker, during which I have provided psychotherapy treatment for female and male molestation survivors of all ages. My specialty includes counseling sexual abuse victims both individually and in groups. In addition, I have provided training on the topic for other professionals as well as the public sector and have written articles on the subject. Through my practice and additional research, I became aware of the inadequacy of services for family and individual counseling for the mothers of molested children and the lack of a thorough understanding of family dynamics that would promote healing for the molested child. This book, based on an informal research study, is one small step toward trying to fill that gap.

As I conducted my taped interviews with these mothers, I learned a great deal as they humbly and bravely shared their stories. I often shared tears with them as I listened. One mother I interviewed said the discovery of a child's molestation is like going to sleep by a campfire only to awaken to a forest fire that's out of control for days. The damage of this fire takes years to repair.

As you understand the world of mothers of molestation survivors, you will learn that MOMS can be very strong, compassionate, and brave. Their stories have made a difference in my life, and I hope they can make a difference in yours too.

Most of the mothers interviewed played a significant role in what happened to their children, especially in the children's recovery process. When a mother supports her child, the healing and recovery occur more quickly and deeply. My goal is to provide understanding regarding the different types of mothers of molestation survivors. Another goal is to educate members of the community about the symptoms of molestation, what to do if you suspect or know that molestation is occurring, and who the perpetrators are. I also offer resources for healing through various types of traditional and non-traditional treatment.

My hope and prayer is that this book will help these mothers find support and become more vocal. MOMS are a group of women that society has overlooked. However, can you imagine the impact these mothers would have if, they united and demanded changes in the education available to the public and private sectors about molestation and championed tougher laws protecting children from perpetrators? Many mothers interviewed for this book were willing to protect their children, no matter the cost. As a mother, you only get one chance to protect your child from molestation.

I am the mother of two children, enabling me to have the heart, mind, soul, and intuition of a mother. I have great empathy for mothers of molestation survivors and the battles they face.

Know that this book is more than my clinical observations and conclusions. Writing this book has been a heartfelt dream.

The names, circumstances, and details of the stories in this book have been altered carefully to protect the mothers, children, siblings, and even perpetrators involved while preserving the stories' essential points. I have chosen to refer predominantly to children as female in this book because most molestation survivors are female. However, the information provided includes male survivors. My reference to "child sexual abuse" refers to a child who is used for an adult's sexual gratification and power. That child could be a male or female from the ages of infant to eighteen. The sexual abuse includes all kinds of sexual mistreatment, including touching and penetration.

This book is divided into four sections, beginning with the description of various types of mothers of molestation survivors. As you progress through the change, healing, and transformation sections, you will better understand who these mothers are and how you can support them. Perhaps you are taking the step to begin your own journey in healing a past trauma. You are very brave and are an important human being deserving of all that is good.

You can help make an impact on the issue of child sexual abuse by educating yourself, starting with this book. Read these words, take to heart what is shared, and spread what you have learned. Join with the mothers of molestation survivors. MOMS can also include fathers, family members, guardians and caregivers.

Thank you for reading and contributing to this effort,

Kim Johnson

SECTION I

UNDERSTANDING

CHAPTER 1

THE PROTECTIVE MOTHER FACING THE BATTLE

When a child reveals to her mother she has been molested, how a mother responds establishes a path of recovery for the child. There are several steps she may or may not take. It is not enough for the mother to believe her daughter: she must also back this belief through actions. Unfortunately, not all mothers do so.

During my research on mothers of molestation survivors, it became clear that there are basically four types of mothers, with some variations: the Protective Mother, the Un-Protective Mother, the Over-Protective Mother, and the Co-Perpetrator Mother. However, it is not unusual for a mom to initially be the Un-Protective mother type, but in time develops into the Protective Mother. This possibility reassures mothers who feel they have not done the right thing in the past that they can be better mothers going forward.

Ideally, a molested child will have a Protective Mother to help her cope and heal from the sexual abuse. The Protective Mother immediately takes the necessary steps to defend her daughter. When she does, the battle begins.

Who is the Protective Mother? This is a story of a mother who exemplifies this role.

MARIA'S STORY

I will always remember the February evening that changed my life forever. We had just arrived home from a family vacation with our friends. We had gone on our annual trip to the mountains over the President's Day holiday where we played in the snow, made snow angels, and ate and laughed together. I was tucking my precious young daughter into bed. As I was about to kiss her and say good night, she did something little girls should not know how to do. She proceeded to put her tongue in my mouth. I was shocked and dumbfounded. The room around me spun as if I had just gotten off the fastest rollercoaster ever made. I stumbled over my words as I tried calmly to ask her to clarify what she had just done. She said, "Daddy does this to me." Questions were flying through my mind, such as WHAT, WHEN, HOW did this happen? Yet inside, I knew there was truth to what she was saying. Looking back there had been suspicious signs of abnormal sexual behavior which my first instinct was to deny. As my sweet daughter looked to me for reassurance, I tried to gain my composure and finish our nightly routine. I comforted her and told her that she would be all right.

As I left her bedroom, I marched down the hallway like a soldier heading to the front line of the battleground. I decided to be honest and tell my husband everything our daughter had just revealed. I confronted him with the horrific details. After more than ten years of marriage, it was the first time he appeared stunned and at a loss for words. As I continued to question him and demand answers, he denied any inappropriate behavior. But I knew in the deepest part of my being that something desperately wrong had occurred. He was caught in one of the darkest acts known in our society. Although he wanted to talk to our daughter, I wouldn't let him approach her. The shock felt as though a loved one had died. I had no one to talk to, nowhere to turn to. The man who was my support, I now viewed as a monster. I cried throughout the night while praying to God to tell me what to do next. I decided then I would do anything to protect our daughter from any further harm, and so my battle began. I knew then that my life would never be the same.

Maria's story is an example of a mother who decides to protect her child. Of course, this story contains several tragedies—a sexually abused daughter, a perpetrator father, and a traumatized mother. Many sexual abuse survivors talked to me during counseling about their mother's response after revealing "the secret" to their mother. How the mother responds to the news that her child has been molested is vital to the child's healing and recovery. This response includes, emotional support and protection from future situations where there is danger of further molestation.

THE PROTECTIVE MOTHER IS RARE.

Unfortunately, most mothers do not or cannot make their child's safety a top priority. The protective mother is rare because so many mothers are unwilling or unable to make the sacrifices necessary to undertake the battle once they learn of the sexual abuse.

The Protective Mother often stands alone with her traumatized child. Frequently, she receives little or no support from family and friends because of their many fears and past experiences. Because molestation is a taboo subject in our society today, MOMS and victims are commonly shunned, which inhibits our progress toward the prevention of molestation. By supporting victims and their families, we will help decrease the stigma surrounding molestation. This, in turn, will give victims and their families courage to find healing through counseling and sharing their stories with others. Because abuse can beget more abuse, this will also be an important step in breaking the cycle of generational molestation.

The number of individuals impacted by sexual assault is overwhelming. Statistics show that between 12 and 35 percent of girls and between 4 and 9 percent of boys are molested sometime during their childhood. However, these statistics will vary depending on factors such as the definitions used in a given survey. Also, as a therapist I have observed very few incidents that are actually reported. This means many MOMS have family and friends who were molested or know of someone who was molested. The average individual does not want to be reminded of his or her traumatic past, so too often, the response is, "I don't want to get involved."

This is another reason the Protective Mother is unusual: many mothers of molestation survivors have some form of molestation in their personal history. If the mother has received treatment and for the most part has healed from her trauma, she is more motivated and better equipped to believe and act on what her child has revealed. However, if she has not begun or has done limited psychological/emotional work on her past, she will be less likely to assist her child. Unfortunately, no reliable statistics currently exist to support the large number of MOMS who have been sexually abused themselves. However, through my research and private practice, I discovered the number is truly larger than one would guess. This leads to the question, "Why would a mother who was molested as a child marry or get involved with a man who would molest her child in a similar way?" While this question can be complicated to answer, mothers who have themselves been sexually abused tend to attract and be attracted to men who feel familiar to them, causing them to repeat patterns in their lives.

THE BATTLE THE PROTECTIVE MOTHER FACES

The Protective Mother faces a fierce battle when she acts on what her child has revealed. Her home is turned upside down regardless of who has hurt her child. Every area of her life is affected—emotionally, psychologically, socially, financially, and legally. Normally, one of the first steps the Protective Mother takes is to report the molestation to the authorities, such as the local Child Protective Services and/or the Police or Sherriff's Department. In some cases, a mandated reporter such as a teacher or child therapist will already have filed a report. A friend, neighbor, or family member can also file such a report. Unfortunately, some MOMS learn what happened to their children via a report someone else completed.

Sometimes it is in the best interest of the child and mother to wait to file a report in order to enable the mother to prepare for future changes. This gives them sufficient time to plan the most beneficial way to confront the perpetrator and have the best possible outcome under the circumstances.

In some instances, a report to the authorities is not filed because the incident is disclosed to church leadership. Allowing church leadership to deal with molestation cases is seldom an effective method because too often they provide insufficient follow-through with discipline and treatment for the parties involved. Even if you have confidence your church would handle the situation appropriately, to ensure accountability, it is best to report suspected molestation to the appropriate outside authorities.

After a report is filed, the Protective Mother must wait to learn whether any action will be taken. It is important to note that when a report is made, it is of "suspected" child abuse, which means the authorities will conduct an investigation. The investigation process can occur immediately if the child is at immanent risk, if not, the investigative process can move slowly. If the alleged perpetrator is the father or a boyfriend who lives in the home, it is very important that the Protective Mother remove him immediately. If she cannot, the authorities usually will do so at her request. If the alleged perpetrator is not removed, Child Protective Services will remove the child from the home for his or her safety.

If the perpetrator lives outside of the home, the mother must assure the authorities that the child will *not* have contact with this person while the case is being investigated. The Protective Mother will have no issue with a policy of "no contact" in fact, this mother usually refuses contact unless it is court ordered.

During this investigation process, the Protective Mother must be assertive in communicating to the authorities on her child's behalf while being careful not to coach her child. In most situations, the child is interviewed by one or more of the following important people related to her case: a school counselor, a social worker from Child Protective Services, a police officer and/or police detective, an interviewer who videotapes the testimony for the District Attorney's Office, and/or a child therapist. Therefore, the child's story must remain *her* story, untainted by adults' additions and interpretations.

CARI'S STORY

It was in the middle of a busy afternoon at work. The phone rang. It was the counselor at my daughter's elementary school. She called to inform me that my daughter had asked to talk with her that morning. As the counselor continued to talk, I wasn't prepared for what she was about to say. She explained my daughter had revealed to her that her stepfather had touched her inappropriately during the night. It had happened more than one time. My daughter had been bothered by it for a long time, and she couldn't keep the secret any longer. She was afraid to talk to me, so a friend of hers had suggested she talk to the school counselor. My daughter had also been afraid of what might happen to her stepfather.

Many questions ran through my mind as I tried to listen closely. What in the world was she talking about? I explained to the counselor I had no knowledge of the situation. The counselor was fairly soft spoken and empathetic, yet direct. She told me as a mandated reporter, she had already called the local child abuse department social services to report what my daughter had disclosed to her. The counselor explained that at minimum I should receive a call from the child abuse department. They may want further information and could possibly interview my daughter. The school counselor ended the call by offering supportive counseling for my daughter. As my heart pounded and my body shook, I hung up the phone, grabbed my personal items, and informed my manager I was leaving immediately due to a family crisis.

On the drive home, I was planning my attack. I first needed to talk to my daughter, who would now be home from school, to find out more information before confronting her stepfather. I kept telling myself to keep my composure, but I wanted to break down and cry. As my daughter bravely answered my questions and shared her story, I knew she was telling the truth because of the details she provided. I tried to be strong for her and did my best to regain my composure and comfort her.

Later that night my husband and I had a major confrontation. He left the house denying any wrongdoing. We had more to discuss as time went on, but it's sufficient to say that the marriage ended that night. Because my husband had left the home, I knew that my daughter was safe. I had done my best to protect her as soon as I found out what happened.

THE PROTECTIVE MOTHER CARES
FOR HER WOUNDED CHILD

After filing the report, the Protective Mother often feels overwhelmed. Her emotional and psychological stamina is tested as her life begins to be in upheaval. The Protective Mother is contending with a traumatized child who is emotionally exhausted after telling her story and answering the same questions to many different professionals involved with their case. The child is also often weary from feeling sad and confused when the father of the perpetrator because there a part of her that misses him even though he hurt her.

Taking care of a traumatized child requires the Protective Mother to be patient, tolerant, accepting, and consistent in dealing with the child's behavior. The child may spontaneously talk in more detail about the abuse through words, play, and/or artwork. For instance, she may draw pictures using dark colors that depict things like a "monster" or someone chasing her. In addition, the child may throw her toys or hit her stuffed animals in anger and confusion. It is healthy for the child to have the freedom to express her thoughts and feelings in such a manner. It is also very healing for the child if her mother enters into her chaotic world by listening to her and encouraging her to talk by asking questions. Some questions the Protective Mother can ask are, "What happened next? What did he tell you? Where were you? How did you feel?" The more thoughts and feelings the child expresses with a nurturing mother, the faster, more effective, and long-term her healing process will be.

As the child talks, it can be terribly painful for the Protective Mother because she is in shock from what she is hearing. Her child's account of the incident can trigger feelings of anger and rage in her. She may even feel like she wants to "kill" the perpetrator for what he did. A few isolated cases exist of a perpetrator being murdered by the mother for his crime. However, it is imperative the Protective Mother understand that if she harms the alleged perpetrator, the child may possibly lose both parents.

In addition to expressing thoughts and feelings, the child may also display unusual behaviors typical of a child who has been sexually violated. It is common for the child to have bad dreams that wake her up in the middle of the night. Of course, the Protective Mother will need to comfort her child after a bad dream. It is therapeutic for the child to talk about the bad dream in the morning, if she remembers it. The child may also become more aggressive in her play with other children. Because she does not know how to appropriately express her anger, she may displace her anger onto another child. The Protective Mother needs to intervene and stop such behavior. However, it is important for the mother to help the child process her anger she can validate the child's feeling and allow the child to appropriately express her anger. This anger issue can be brought to the child's therapist as well. In addition to anger issues, the child may exhibit other problems at school. This may include, getting distracted easily, not completing assignments, or feeling unmotivated. It is helpful for the Protective Mother to be aware of these potential issues and communicate regularly with the teacher to follow up on any problems. Additional symptoms a molested child may exhibit will be discussed in Chapter 5.

The Protective Mother may also feel overwhelmed by the legal issues raised by her child's abuse. It is highly recommended that the Protective Mother keep a detailed log of dates, times, and details the child shares with her mother. This information is invaluable not only for legal purposes, but also for sharing with the child's therapist. As time passes, it is also helpful to remember important information for personal reasons.

THE PROTECTIVE MOTHER

While the mother's role is to support the child, she needs to find ways to take care of herself. Most importantly, she needs to cope with her own pain by talking to a supportive person enabling her to express her deep sorrow and loss of her child's innocence. However, often the Protective Mother may feel alone, with no one to turn to. While she may long for someone to give her support, it is important to remember she must be very careful whom she confided in about her child's sexual assault. Unfortunately, this is to protect the entire family from being ostracized. It is not uncommon for the Protective Mother to be publicly blamed for what happened. When too many adults—including school staff, neighbors, and friends—learn of the abuse, the child is commonly labeled and excluded from events. Although one might think the child's ordeal would inspire others to treat her with kindness, the opposite is more often the case. The MOMS I interviewed frequently said that when other parents would learn of her child's sexual abuse, those parents feared their own child would be at risk. Hence, the Protective Mother must use wisdom when sharing her story.

LAURA'S STORY

In the darkest part of the night, I remember lying in my bed sobbing into my pillow while hoping not to wake my kids. My eyes would be swollen in the morning from all the tears I shed the night before. My gut would ache from the anguish. My heart was shattered into a million pieces. My sobs would be deep, long, and hard as I thought of what he had done to my child. I had done everything right. I waited to have a baby until after I was married, we owned our home, my career was established, and there was money in bank.

Now I had so many questions that couldn't be answered. How could he hurt our child? She was so young, innocent, and fragile. What was he thinking? Didn't he realize what he was doing? Didn't he think he would get caught? Who was this monster I was married to? I had trusted him with everything, including our precious daughter. I wanted to scream, yell, and kick him. I wanted him to hurt like he had hurt my daughter and me. I had to believe there was a special place in Hell for him!

I cried out to God. WHY did this happen? Where were you? My faith was being tested to its very core. During those dark nights, I hung onto all

I knew, which was God. I believed He had not deserted me. I knew He saw my pain. God didn't want this to happen to either of us. I believed that even though I didn't have the answers to my questions, somehow, some way, God was my hope in this madness.

When the Protective Mother is hearing and observing all the thoughts, feelings, and behaviors of her troubled child, it is essential for her to have a couple of trusted friends or family members who will listen to her talk about what has happened. The friend or family member may hear the same story over and over, which can be frustrating, but repeating the story is how the Protective Mother processes the tragedy. When a Protective Mother receives emotional support, it empowers her to carry on fighting for her wounded child. It is difficult for the Protective Mother to begin her own psychological treatment at this point because she is contending with stabilizing her child's mental wellness and all of her other responsibilities. In addition to offering emotional support, friends can assist a Protective Mother in many other ways. This could include, taking care of the child, helping with household chores and repairs, and/or assisting with legal preparations.

While conducting interviews with MOMS, I was stunned by how often Protective Mothers longed for support from other Protective Mothers. In general protective mothers live in isolation. These women consistently expressed how much they would benefit from talking to other Protective Mothers in their situation. One sexual abuse survivor I interviewed said, "You have my full approval to use my story. I wish my mom had your support back then!" to connect Protective Mothers so they can face the battle of child sexual assault with support, encouragement, and empowerment.

THE PROTECTIVE MOTHER FACES THE SOCIAL BATTLE

Unfortunately, as family, friends, and neighbors learn of the traumatic situation, they often react poorly. Because the topic of sexual abuse is taboo in our society and most people already have some type of disturbing experience with sexual abuse, they often find it too scary or painful to provide support to those who need it most. It takes a strong, secure, and accepting person to stand by the Protective Mother throughout this battle. It is not a matter of true friendship, but of being incredibly flexible, diligent, and caring enough to be there consistently for the mother for the full year or two it can take before some equilibrium is restored to the lives of the Protective Mother and her child.

If the perpetrator is the father, stepfather, or live-in boyfriend, his relatives often support him and withdraw from the Protective Mother. If the mother was close to his family, this withdrawal can be a huge loss for her. On the other hand, sometimes it can be a relief. In either case, it is not unusual for the perpetrator's family to pressure her to withdraw the case and change what she has said about his involvement in the situation. To this end, they can be verbally and emotionally aggressive toward her. Furthermore, if the perpetrator or his family previously provided any financial support, it is generally discontinued, resulting in financial concerns for the mother. Friends or neighbors who were close to the perpetrator may also distance themselves from the Protective Mother or pressure her to recant the accusation. Thus, taking a stand in this battle has enormous social ramifications for the Protective Mother.

As the Protective Mother discusses the sexual abuse with family members and friends, she is usually asked whether she knew her child was being sexually abused. In interviewing MOMS who had themselves been molested, I found some of them genuinely believed their mothers had no idea at the time that they were being abused by their fathers, stepfathers, or mothers' live-in boyfriends. Other women believed their mothers had known about the abuse; then the question as to why their mothers did not stop the abuse is raised. Often, the mother did not know how to prove that abuse was taking place and feared the fallout of making the accusation.

When a mother suspects or learns her child is being sexually abused, the most important action is what the mother does next. If she has suspicions but no proof her child is being molested, it is better for her to do something rather than nothing. In Chapter 5, the topic of suspicion will be reviewed in detail and guidelines will be provided for what a mother can do.

EMMA'S STORY

I was only six years old when I lost my innocence.
We were at my aunt's house visiting. My cousin
was sixteen years old and had molested me several
times before my mother caught him in the act. I'll

never forget my mom's reaction as she screamed at him to stop. Then she marched out of the bedroom, straight to her sister, and confronted her. A huge altercation took place between my mom and my aunt. While comforting me, my mom quickly packed our bags, and we left. My mom and her sister had very little contact after this horrendous incident. My aunt refused to believe my mother, even though my mother had walked in on her son hurting me. I was never molested by him again. My mom decided to keep the situation in the family, and there was no police involvement.

The Protective Mother can suffer from lost family relationships, as in Emma's story. Another woman I interviewed told of how she lost a friend after confiding about her daughter's molestation by her own husband. The friend told the Protective Mother the incident surely could not have happen as she thought, even if it had, she could get over it. The friend went on to explain her father had molested her as a child, but she believed she had come out of the situation just fine. Her mother didn't leave her father, so why should the Protective Mother leave her husband? The friend thought it was best for the Protective Mother to stay with her husband because her daughter "needed" her father to be around, and concluded by saying she could not be the Protective Mother's friend any longer unless she reconciled with her husband. The Protective Mother felt so betrayed that she never contacted that friend again.

While there are different degrees of friendship, in the arena of sexual assault, a friend or family member is either "in" or "out." Sometimes, after the crisis is over and equilibrium is restored in the lives of the Protective Mother and the sexually abused child, the Protective Mother can rebuild relationships with the sympathetic family and friends who couldn't bring themselves to be there during the hardship. She has matured enough to understand that only a few are able to provide support during this battle. While some relationships can be healed over time, through this process, the Protective Mother will learn who her true friends, family and supporters are.

THE PROTECTIVE MOTHER FACES THE FINANCIAL BATTLE

The Protective Mother struggles with many financial issues. Since sexual abuse crosses all socioeconomic boundaries, persons of all income brackets are impacted financially in one way or another. If the perpetrator is removed from the home either by the Protective Mother or through legal means, divorce usually follows, and the perpetrator will commonly retaliate by withholding financial support for the mortgage, rent, utilities, food, and/or child support. As a result the Protective Mother often loses the home she created.

If the Protective Mother has not been working outside the home, she often must now find a way to provide an income. She may have to become creative, whether that means cashing in assets, borrowing money from family or friends, selling items, or using a credit line. If the Protective Mother does work outside the home, she is more financially independent.

In addition to existing household expenses, the Protective Mother now has expenses such as counseling fees for the child and herself, increased childcare costs, and legal fees such as payment to a divorce attorney. If the Protective Mother isn't accustomed to overseeing the family budget, paying bills, and financial planning, she may need advice and direction. Her primary focus should be establishing financial stability and independence for herself and her child.

If the perpetrator already lives outside the home, the financial impact is likely to be less severe. However, legal fees and counseling costs may still exist. In researching this book, I discovered a few cases where adult survivors who were molested as children received financial reparation for pain and suffering from the perpetrator. However, these cases were rare, and the payments came too late to help them through the most financially difficult period resulting from the perpetrator's crime.

It is important to remember that money, though necessary, is of less importance than the safety, recovery, and healing of the molested child and her mother. The Protective Mother does not let financial difficulties stop her, even if fighting the battle means losing her home. She has learned that it is people who make a home, not the building itself, and she seeks to ensure that only trustworthy people are invited into the homemaking process going forward.

THE PROTECTIVE MOTHER FACES
THE LEGAL BATTLE

Finally, the Protective Mother is affected as the case moves through the legal system. When a child reveals to a police officer or police detective that he or she has been sexually assaulted, an investigation is begun. Identifying a single "standard" model for such investigations is difficult, since each may be very complex and may proceed differently depending on the specific details of the case. Most counties have a formal process where a child is videotaped by a person specially trained to interview children who have been molested. The interviewer asks very specific, objective questions about the incident(s). Unfortunately, in these situations, children often freeze and are unable to talk. Sometimes the child is too young to communicate complex events effectively, so his or her story is too confusing or does not provide enough details for an effective legal case, which the perpetrator knows. When the child is able to provide a more substantial account, the investigation is more likely to continue. The tape is then normally reviewed by someone from the District Attorney's Office. If the child's story is substantiated by a medical exam which documents damage consistent with sexual assault, this strengthens the case considerably. However, for a number of reasons, not every case will have such medical evidence.

If the child's statement, medical examination (when applicable), and other sources provide enough evidence for a conviction, the perpetrator is charged and the trial process begins. At times, the case does not go to trial because the perpetrator plea bargains with the District Attorney's Office, meaning he pleads guilty in exchange for a lesser sentence. If the perpetrator is convicted, he may serve time in jail or prison. After the perpetrator is released, there are probation requirements and long-term ramifications for his actions. In many states, the perpetrator is required to register as a sex offender and is not allowed to reside near schools, parks, and other places where children congregate. Unfortunately, I learned from interviewing MOMS that it is unusual for a conviction to take place, because many cases lack sufficient evidence. It is very difficult to convict when it is just the child's word against the perpetrator's word.

Fortunately for vigilant parents, convictions of perpetrators are recorded in public records. The website, www.MegansLaw. com lists the descriptions, home addresses, and specific crimes of registered sex offenders. The website is named for a law passed in

1995 after Megan Kanka, a young New Jersey girl, was raped and murdered by a neighbor who had been convicted of aggravated sexual assault on a child. No one in the neighborhood had known that this neighbor was a convicted pedophile. Thanks to the law, it is now easy to discover whether a sex offender lives nearby. While these lists allow parents to protect their children, it is important to keep this information in balance with reality: be aware of the danger, but don't live in fear.

Here's the story of one mother who was new to a neighborhood:

SARAH'S STORY

I had befriended an older couple in the town we had recently moved to. I was a single mother, and I didn't have family around to help with the children. Over time, this older couple became surrogate grandparents for my kids. One evening, I allowed this couple to watch my daughter overnight. They lived close by, and I felt I knew them well. I trusted them. However, the next day after picking my daughter up from their house, she commented that the man "touched my stomach." I asked her some questions, and most importantly, I listened to her. She felt uncomfortable with the man who helped watch her. I confronted the couple and the wife begged me not to call the police, perhaps because of a previous conviction. I stopped the relationship with them, and I never communicated with them again.

The legal processes both a sexual abuse survivor and perpetrator must undergo can be very stressful for the Protective Mother. She must support her child as the child is interviewed. She must not coach the child in any way, yet encourage him or her to speak the truth about what happened. Reassuring her child frequently that he or she is not at fault for anything that happened is vital. The child needs to understand that whatever happens to the perpetrator is a consequence of his actions alone, not the child's, and it is not the child's job to protect the perpetrator. At the same time, when a bond previously existed between the child and perpetrator, the child may miss him, and she needs to be able to express this feeling. The child's feelings about the lost relationship can be very difficult for the Protective Mother. In this situation, the Protective Mother must use her support systems to express her frustrations.

After a perpetrator father has served time and complied with the court's requirements, such as intensive psychological treatment, he may be allowed contact with his child again. When cases go through the family court system rather than the criminal law court system, different evaluations may be made to determine what happened and what form of future contact, if any, the father may have with his child. As a result of the findings, certain requirements are set in place, such as supervised visitation between the father and child. This reunification can be very difficult for the Protective Mother, especially if she still has unresolved feelings about the father. Her best ammunition is to safeguard her child by educating her and by keeping communication open with her. Methods of safeguarding the child will be discussed in Chapter 5.

Various agencies exist to help the entire family through the reunification process. At times, the Protective Mother is able to forgive her husband for hurting their child, and through the help of very specialized therapy, families are reunited. However, it takes a unique Protective Mother to be able to go through this process, even in those cases where the perpetrator is repentant and willing to change his behavior.

SUMMARY

Who is the Protective Mother? In the end, the Protective Mother is a unique woman. She has the incredible strength to survive one of the most horrific crimes that can occur in her child's life and the tenacity to endure long-suffering. Without a Protective Mother, these wounded children would have little hope. Through the mother's monumental efforts, healing can take place. The Protective Mother is more rare and valuable than the finest, purest diamond. Through her hardships, she exemplifies how important it is never to give up. The Protective Mother may go unnoticed, but through her integrity and strength she will rise above the ordeal. She will fight the battle no matter the cost. She may even be YOU.

EXERCISE

Can you think of a mother who protected her child? If so, what happened?

____

____

____

____

____

If necessary, did your mother take steps to protect you? What happened? If your mother did not take steps to protect you, what occurred?

____

____

____

____

____

Are you a mother currently in a situation where you need to protect your child? If so, what do you think you need to do?

____

____

____

____

____

CHAPTER 2

THE UN-PROTECTIVE MOTHER RUNNING FROM THE BATTLE

In this chapter, we will learn about the Un-Protective Mother, who does NOT enter the battle. When this mother becomes aware that her child is or has been sexually abused, she makes very little effort to help her child, or does nothing at all. Un-Protective Mothers have many reasons why they do not respond to their children's cries for help. Ultimately, these mothers avoid the situation because they feel the battle is too overwhelming. Why doesn't a mother do everything in her power to protect her child? Who is the Un-Protective Mother?

Let's begin by looking at the story of an un-protective mother.

CYNTHIA'S STORY

I was so afraid of him. I would regularly see my father beat my mom. He hurt me as well— in the bedroom. He threatened to kill my mother if I revealed our secret to her. He also sexually abused my older sister. Although my sister's sexual abuse came out when my parents divorced, mine did not. I held my anger in silence for years as my mother seemed to ignore the possibility that I too had been abused. When my abuse was revealed many years later, I learned that my mother felt "He would never touch the baby." Underneath the denial, my mom had suppressed her gut feeling I had been a victim. She had convinced herself it hadn't happened to me. My mom lived in constant fear, perhaps for her life and the life of her children. After seeking therapy, I now understand because of the trauma of domestic violence she was not able to speak out to protect herself or her children. I finally learned "she did the best she could with what she had."

Through my research, I discerned that there are six basic reasons why Un-Protective Mothers do nothing to protect their children:

- Domestic Violence
- Low Self-Esteem
- Substance Abuse
- Personal History
- Lack of Resources
- Illness

DOMESTIC VIOLENCE

Domestic violence is a major cause of why mothers don't protect their children. In these situations, the mother is fighting for her life. The Un-Protective Mother tiptoes around, trying her best not to upset the rage-filled, violent husband/boyfriend. While her partner becomes more and more agitated, she works harder and harder to calm him down by trying to prevent anything that may upset him. This may include meals that are late, a dirty house, or noisy kids. All the while, she awaits the next abusive episode, even though he promised many times never to hurt her again. The Un-Protective Mother thinks about escaping him, but she finds herself unable to carry out her plans. Sometimes she is familiar with this horrific situation because she previously witnessed her mother contend with physical violence. She promised herself she wouldn't tolerate the abuse her mother did, yet she finds herself in the same place. Statistics demonstrate it takes an average of seven attempts for a woman to leave a domestic violence relationship before she finally breaks free.

It is understandable why a child can be sexually abused in this situation. Most violent men have little or no respect for the women they hurt. In fact, they are usually angry and hate women in general. They do what they want when they want, so what would stop them from hurting a child as well as a woman? Since the Un-Protective Mother is dealing with her own abuse and fighting to stay alive in most cases, she is unaware of her child's abuse. If she does suspect her child is being abused, she commonly doesn't investigate it because she fears her husband's retribution upon her (or the children) for interfering. In some cases, however, it is one thing for the mother to tolerate being abused, and quite another when she learns he is hurting her child. She then finds the courage to do something and fight the battle!

LOW SELF-ESTEEM

The Un-Protective Mother may also run from the battle of protecting her child because she lacks self-esteem. This Un-Protective Mother too has been "beaten up," but in another way. She has little or no sense of self. She lacks self-respect, self-love, and self-pride. For most of her life, she has received negative messages about herself by the most important people in her life-parents, authority figures, boyfriends, or husbands such as, "You're no good," "You can't do anything right," and "You're stupid." She has learned not only to believe these awful comments, but to define herself by them. Consequently, she will tolerate a lot that a woman with healthy self-esteem would never dream of allowing. The Un-Protective Mother is so desperate to be loved and accepted that she will even sacrifice her child.

The following is a story of how a mother's low self-esteem prevented her from protecting her daughter:

TAMMY'S STORY

The hold my stepfather had on my mother was stronger than the bond between my mom and me. She would do anything for him because she defined herself as he saw her. As long as she was with him, her life had meaning and purpose. When my sexual abuse was revealed, my mother told me it was entirely my fault. As a five-year-old little girl, I had been running around in a tee shirt and bathing suit one afternoon while playing in the water. Unbeknownst to me my stepfather became inappropriately aroused while watching me. Because of my mother's insecurities, she became furious with me. In a rage, she blurted out that she regretted I had been born and wished that I would leave and live with my grandparents.

Although I was emotionally broken, I stayed with my mother and stepfather until I was sixteen at which time I got pregnant and married the baby's father whom I loved. Unfortunately, as a child I had been desperate to be loved, and my mother had misplaced blame and failed to protect an innocent child because of her low self-esteem. My mom is still with my stepfather, however, I've decided to put the past behind me.

SUBSTANCE ABUSE

By abusing alcohol, prescription drugs, marijuana, or street drugs, the Un-Protective Mother numbs herself. She, therefore, cannot battle clearly and effectively. It is also quite common for the perpetrator to be drinking or using a substance when he is sexually abusing a child. This mother often drinks or uses substances, either with or without the perpetrator. Because of the effects of these substances, the Un-Protective Mother becomes less functional and the child becomes more vulnerable.

Here is the story of a mother whose substance abuse prevented her from protecting her child:

SUSAN'S STORY

It was the early 1970's, a time of sexual discovery, and my mom was a free spirit and very promiscuous. It was very common for my mother and her girlfriends to drink and talk openly about their sex lives while I was in the same room. One day she became angry when I would not leave the room and commented I could not possibly know what they were talking about. I told her that in fact I did know. When she asked me more questions, I was too embarrassed to answer so I wrote her a letter and gave it to her. I didn't use the right words, but I described sexual acts to her. She wanted to know how I knew these things. I told her I talked about them with my girlfriends, but she did not believe me. After her continuous questions, I told her what her boyfriend had been doing to me. In a drunken rage, she yelled at me to stay the hell away from him. Years later when my mother and I talked about the sexual abuse by her boyfriend, her memory of how she responded was very different than mine. My mother had not protected me as a child due to her drunken state at the time.

PERSONAL HISTORY

While interviewing mothers for this book, I was stunned by the high percentage of mothers who were themselves sexually abused as children. When a mother has not dealt with her own history of abuse, it gravely impacts her ability to respond to her child's sexual abuse. If a mother tries to pretend her sexual abuse never occurred, the problem becomes magnified when she learns of her child's molestation. In some cases, the Un-Protective Mother does not want to recognize her child's trauma because it commonly triggers memories she has repressed of what happened to her as a child. Suddenly, she is faced with both situations. Conversely, when a mother has already sought treatment for her own childhood sexual abuse, she is able to respond more positively and proactively with her child. Interestingly, I've noted over the years of providing treatment to MOMS that their children are often hurt in a similar manner and at a similar age.

This is a story of how three generations in a family experienced sexual abuse.

EVAN'S STORY

My grandmother was in her nineties when she and my mother were watching a television show about child sexual abuse. This prompted my grandmother to tell my mom about her own memories of being sexually abused as a child. This was the first time she had ever acknowledged her abuse. Ironically, I was sexually abused by my grandfather. When I told my mom what her father had done to me, she was shocked. She believed me, but it was very difficult for her to think of her father as a perpetrator. It was difficult for my mom to put those pieces of the puzzle together, but she did. She responded positively by taking a part-time teaching job to be able to pay for my counseling. It was hard for her to come to terms with her family history, but she did the best she could to support me in my recovery.

LACK OF RESOURCES

When a mother faces the battle of protecting her child after a sexual assault, it requires all of her resources to fight. Frequently, mothers are Un-Protective because they lack financial and social resources. At times, mothers stay with the perpetrator because they fear they cannot afford to live on their own with their children. The mother may be a stay-at-home mom who hasn't worked outside the home for years. She lacks the skills to find a job and may not have the assets to move out and support a household. She may not have family or friends who will support her financially or emotionally. Often, she finds herself isolated and alone, and the stigma of sexual abuse adds to her trauma.

ILLNESS

Some physical illnesses can weaken a mother so much that all of her energy goes into getting well. This Un-Protective Mother is consumed with medical appointments and hospital stays and is preoccupied with searching for a cure to her illness. She is often bedridden and unavailable. An Un-Protective Mother may also have a mental illness, including severe depression, which makes it difficult for her to handle basic tasks in her life. In especially severe mental health cases, she is unavailable because she is committed to a psychiatric hospital. If this mother refuses her psychiatric medications, the psychiatric disorder can worsen and cause additional problems. I found that it was common for these mothers to be in and out of any hospital which provided an opportunity for the perpetrator to molest the child.

Here is one story of how a mother's illness hampered her ability to protect her child:

KATIE'S STORY

My mom was pregnant with my brother when she began having premature labor and was ordered by her physician to be on bed rest. My mom was on special medication to stop the contractions. I was five years old at the time but remember family and friends helping out. My dad had to spend extra time taking care of me and this is when the abuse began. Months after my brother was born, I told my mom what my dad was doing to me. She said that she was too tired to talk and I was imagining things.

SUMMARY

The Un-Protective Mother does not protect her child for many reasons: domestic violence, low self-esteem, substance abuse, her past history of abuse, lack of financial and social resources, and physical or mental illness. Although these are difficult situations, they are not hopeless if the Un-Protective mother chooses to get help.

EXERCISE

· · · · · · · · ·

Can you think of an example of an Un-Protective Mother? Maybe you personally know such a mother or can think of one from a movie or a book. What happened to her and her child?

____

____

____

____

____

Which of the reasons listed in this chapter caused the mother you identified above to be an Un-Protective Mother?

____

____

____

____

____

What would you want to say to the Un-Protective Mother to encourage her to become a Protective Mother?

____

____

____

____

____

CHAPTER 3

THE OVER-PROTECTIVE MOTHER FEARING THE BATTLE

Who is the Over-Protective Mother? The Over-Protective Mother is scared, and out of fear, she desperately over-protects her child. This mother hides from the battle because she is afraid of it. She does her best to hide her child from the terror and potential harm of the outside world. Her world is calculated, and she has designed rules, schedules, and a structure to protect her child. Her goal in life is to prevent her child from ever being hurt.

How does she over-protect her child? The Over-Protective Mother prohibits her child from doing many activities outside of the home, such as spending the night at a friend's house, going away to a church camp, or dating as a teenager. If her child does attend an event, it must be adequately supervised to meet her overly stringent standards. Because the Over-Protective Mother wants to be assured of the safety of the situation, she will often involve herself in any activity outside the house. For example, she will be the Girl Scout troop leader or the team mother for the soccer team. Additionally, the Over-Protective Mother will check out the families of any friends. They must meet her strict criteria and "prove" to be safe. Then the child's friend is invited to their home. Finally, the child may go to her friend's home after a significant period of time in which the friend and family earn the Over-Protective Mother's trust. Similarly, the Over-Protective Mother will closely monitor the music her child listens to, the television programs and movies she watches, any websites she dares to visit, and any communication with friends via the computer, telephone and/or social media. If the Over-Protective Mother believes anything inappropriate has happened or may happen in these situations, she will not allow the child to continue that activity. Hence, the child is raised in a safe cocoon. However, when it comes time to let the butterfly go, the child is unprepared for what's ahead.

The Over-Protective Mother doesn't educate her child regarding friendships with males, the development of her sexuality or dating because "these topics aren't discussed." They are taboo. In fact, little or no communication exists between the Over-Protective Mother and her child regarding sexual matters. Sometimes these topics are overviewed but briefly and with minimal detail. Little conversation or opportunity exists for the child to ask questions, because the Over-Protective mother's obvious negative opinion of the topic makes the child feel very uncomfortable. Consequently, the child is poorly educated leaving her vulnerable and naïve. This situation sets up a "perfect storm" because the unprepared child is more easily taken advantage of by sexual predators that recognize her vulnerability which is exactly what the Over-Protective Mother worked so hard to avoid.

THE OVER-PROTECTIVE MOTHER CREATES AN ACTING-OUT CHILD

As a child grows, it is developmentally necessary for her to challenge her mother in order to develop as an individual. However, the Over-Protective Mother doesn't allow this behavior because of her fears. As a result, the child can become overly rebellious and severely act out against the Over-Protective Mother. For example, she may learn to be sneaky and hide things from her mother or may blatantly act out verbally or through actions. Through her extreme attempt to escape her mother's restrictions, the child finds herself in dangerous situations where she can be sexually abused. Because of her inability to talk to the Over-Protective Mother, the child turns to her peers or other adults for information or help. Frequently, the information she receives is incorrect which results in her being harmed further.

THE OVER-PROTECTIVE MOTHER CREATES A DEPENDENT CHILD

The Over-Protective Mother's child can behave in the extreme opposite to the rebellious child. She rarely leaves the house choosing instead to stay at home where it is comfortable, safe, and secure. She becomes overly dependent on her mother and is fearful of the outside world like her mother. She likes the peace and warmth of the environment her mother has created. This child learns to please others even at the cost of suppressing her own feelings, needs, or wants. She is compliant and a high achiever in the world the Over-Protective Mother has created. Both mother and child are content, for now. However, the child's overly-compliant (and thus easily manipulated) personality makes her just as vulnerable in many ways as risky behavior does. In addition, if the child ever grows up enough to leave the house, the separation can be difficult and painful.

Here is the story of what happened to one woman who grew up with an Over-Protective Mother:

BARBIE'S STORY

I was raised in a conservative, middle-class family. I attended Catholic school from kindergarten through my senior year of high school. I was raised in the same house and neighborhood from an early age until I left for college. In fact, my mother still lives in that house. My family members were filled with anxiety. We were too close, yet there were certain topics we avoided - especially anything about sex.

At age twenty-two, I was living in a large metropolitan city where I was an actor in a play. A fellow actor invited me out on a date. Later that evening, I asked him into my apartment so we could talk and get to know each other better. However, his intentions were different. He kept asking me to have sex and trying slowly to coerce me into it. After denying his advances, he held me down and raped me.

A few weeks later, I found out I was pregnant. I didn't know what to do. My mother and I had never talked about this subject when I was growing up. I felt I had nowhere to go for advice so I made what I thought was the best decision at the time which was to have an abortion.

The abortion was very traumatic because it went against my personal and spiritual values.

I didn't tell my mother about the rape and abortion until I was thirty-eight years old! That was fourteen years later. I was in a position where I had to tell her because of a show I was doing that involved telling my story in order to help other young women. How could I tell the audience my story when I hadn't even told my mother?

To make recovery more difficult, I was treated for the wrong disorder after seeking medical and psychological help. I was treated for anxiety rather than trauma. I did confront my perpetrator on the phone as part of my healing process. At first, he admitted what he had done was wrong, but later he called back and denied any wrongdoing. Yet, I realize he knows that what he did was wrong. He's an animal in his own cage, and I am free. After this realization, my lengthy recovery was finally complete after I bravely told my mother of my past. Her response was amazing. She said, "I can't believe you went through all of this alone." Over the years my mother knew something was wrong, but if she asked me questions I told her I was okay and denied any problems.

Looking back, it would have been very helpful if my mother and I had been able to talk about these issues. The road may have been a little easier. My hope is to prevent other young women from making the mistakes I did. Hopefully, mothers will educate themselves and their children so there is open communication about sensitive subjects.

CHILDREN NEED PAIN TO GROW

In conducting the interviews for this book, I discovered the Over-Protective Mother in particular was often molested as a child. She is determined never to allow her child to suffer a similar assault. However, her efforts to protect often backfire. The problem often arises from the Over-Protective Mother being so extremely protective that she does not want her child to be hurt in any way. However, people need some pain and hurt to help them grow emotionally and psychologically, whether they are children or adults.

Following is the story of how one mother realized her over protective behavior ended up being detrimental to her children:

VIRGINIA'S STORY

We didn't talk about sex growing up because it wasn't "proper." When I was eighteen my dad crossed the line. He violated my sexual boundaries two times by inappropriately touching me. When my sister was about fourteen years old, I found out later, he had tried to French kiss her passionately, but because of her strong self-image she was able to prevent any further abuse from him. We were told by our parents that "counseling is for crazy people," so I never received counseling until I was in my fifties. What I learned in counseling was I had made sure my two children were not hurt as I had been growing up. As a consequence, I smothered them to keep them from any harm. Because of this fear, my husband and I never went out to dinner and left our children with a babysitter. Now both of my adult children have problems in relationships. They are afraid to interact with others. I have come to learn there is value in being uncomfortable; in fact, it can be damaging to kids if they aren't allowed to be uncomfortable. I understand now kids need to be hurt in order to develop and grow emotionally. Over protecting my children was a direct result of the sexual abuse I endured from my father and not being able to learn about appropriate sexual behavior.

<u>47</u>

SUMMARY

The Over-Protective Mother attempts to protect her child by avoiding the battle. She creates an environment she can completely control a fortress that she believes is protected from any harm. When danger occurs, she is unable to leave that fortress to rescue her child despite her child's cries for help. Although the Over-Protective Mother is motivated by love and compassion for her child, her need to protect gets out of hand. Her child is not allowed to do many age-appropriate activities unless the Over-Protective Mother is assured beyond any reasonable standard that the activities are safe. The child may rebel and act out, thereby putting herself in greater danger. More frequently, the child may recoil into her own protective world. Either way, the child is at greater risk for sexual harm due to the Over-Protective Mother's issues.

EXERCISE

Can you think of an example of an Over-Protective Mother? Do you have a friend who had a mother who wouldn't let her participate in normal activities? What happened to her?

____

____

____

____

____

Did the child of the Over-Protective Mother rebel and act out against her mother or did she retreat and become unsociable?

____

____

____

____

What would you say to the Over-Protective Mother so she can understand that her child can gain from pain and NEEDS to be educated regarding sex?

____

____

____

____

____

CHAPTER 4

THE CO-PERPETRATOR MOTHER MANIPULATING THE BATTLE

The Co-Perpetrator Mother avoids the battle just as the Un-Protective Mother does. However, this mother is abusive to her child. Often the Co-Perpetrator Mother has been abused as a child or has had some other significant childhood trauma which in turn has taught her to become abusive. When this mother learns about her daughter's sexual abuse she may or may not do anything about it. This decision is based on how she believes she might benefit from the situation. In other words, this mother uses her child's sexual assault to meet her own needs thereby adding trauma to the child's sexual abuse. She needs to be STOPPED - but it's not the child's job to stop her.

Who is the Co-Perpetrator Mother? How and why would she manipulate the battle to her own advantage rather than protect her child?

NARCISSISM

It is hard to imagine a mother would take advantage of her child's sexual abuse, yet the Co-Perpetrator Mother does so to gain various types of attention for her including sympathy, financial resources, and assistance in caring for her child. The Co-Perpetrator Mother tends to be narcissistic: the world revolves around her. Often she sees her children as objects solely to benefit her in some way. The child's task is to meet the mother's needs rather than the mother meeting the child's needs. If the child's abuse will bring the Co-Perpetrator Mother any attention, resources, or support, the Co-Perpetrator Mother allows and even encourages that abuse.

Here is the story of one woman whose mother played the co-perpetrator role.

SUZANNE'S STORY

My mom was married to her second husband when I was three years old. At that time my stepfather, who I thought of as a bear, would come into my bedroom at night and molest me. He molested my brother and half-brother as well. Although I believe my mother knew, she never questioned me or my brothers, and the abuse continued.

When I was eight, I was playing with my brother one day when he asked me to push him in his wagon. After I refused, he threatened to tell mom about the sexual abuse by our stepfather. I ran ahead of him to the house and told Mom in detail about his nightly visits to our bedrooms. She started to scream hysterically and yell, "How could you do this to me?" She made me feel as though I had done something to her! Shortly after she complained to the family she had a nervous breakdown, and we were to live with our grandparents and uncles so she could recover.

They all knew about the abuse, but no one talked to us or bothered to find counseling for us. My mother inherited money but never offered to use it for counseling for us children. My mom never said she was sorry this had happened to us, or she was sorry for any part she might have had in it. Eventually, my mother and stepfather divorced. To get sympathy for herself, she told people the story of our molestation by her ex-husband, and the trauma had caused her to have a nervous breakdown. She thought of herself only and acted as if she were the victim.

To make matters worse, one year after the divorce, my previous stepfather came for a "visit" and dinner with my mom. He stayed overnight with my mom in our apartment. My mom left early for work the next morning and left me alone in the apartment with him. He told me to come into the bedroom with him. However, I ran into the bathroom to get dressed and left the apartment immediately. I can't believe my mother would put me in this situation in order to have her sexual needs met by this man. I believe she had babies to keep a man around until she grew tired of him. My mother truly lived for herself.

Here is another story in which a mother acts as a co-perpetrator to gain attention.

GINGER'S STORY

My sister's third husband called to tell my mother that my sister was on a business trip and had again left him alone with their vulnerable daughter for a few days. He was taunting my mother because she was aware of the sexual abuse that was taking place by him while my sister would be out of town.

I felt like I met my real mom for the first time when she called to tell me of this situation. She knew about her granddaughter's abuse, but she did nothing about it. She had never shared this information with my sister but wanted empathy and attention from me for being in the middle of a horrible situation. I was in shock that she appeared not to care about the welfare of her granddaughter's safety. How could my mother use this horrific situation to gain attention?

INAPPROPRIATE BOUNDARIES

The Co-Perpetrator Mother may also have inappropriate boundaries with her daughter, but in subtle ways. In one case, a mother bought lingerie for her teenage daughter. The daughter became pregnant and married shortly after she graduated from high school. Yet this mother was surprised her daughter had gotten pregnant and did not know she had contributed to condoning sexual activity at a young age. Another example of inappropriate sexual guidelines is when a mother allows her teenage daughter to befriend or date men who are three to five years older and sexually experienced. Because of her young daughter's innocence, she may develop distorted views of what a healthy physical relationship entails. In addition, this situation can cause a young woman to be at risk for sexual assault, especially if she does not understand the ramifications of dating older men.

GRACE'S STORY

I was fourteen years old. I began talking with a twenty six year old single man who lived down the street. I told this man of my interest in learning how to use hand held radios, and he promised to teach me what I wanted to learn. My mother allowed me to spend time with him. He would take me to the movies where he kissed me and praised my sexual abilities. I remember feeling very good about myself, and I wanted to be sexually desired. The same year, I dated a man who was nineteen. Although I told my mother he was seventeen, she never checked his age or his family background. I learned very quickly that older men were more fun because they had money, a car, their own apartment for sexual activity, and freedom. My mother gave me the freedom of an adult when I was a teenager. My mother did not discourage these relationships, and she failed to teach me appropriate sexual boundaries. Because of her narcissistic life style choices, she did little to protect me.

SUMMARY

When a mother uses her child's abuse for her own gain, she is also a predator. A mother's responsibility is to protect and nurture her child, NOT to use the child for her own benefit. The Co-Perpetrator Mother is mentally ill and weak. She is defined by selfishness and manipulation and can only see what she will gain. Her goal in life is to please herself even if it means risk to her own child.

Most children who have a self-seeking mother develop a "narcissistic wound", consequently, they benefit from learning from another source they do have value and are worthy of love. This wound can be healed when they believe they are precious human beings who deserve to be loved appropriately.

If you know a child who has a Co-Perpetrator Mother, love her. She so very much deserves to be loved.

EXERCISE

Can you think of an example of a Co-Perpetrator Mother? Was she narcissistic?

____

____

____

____

____

How is the child of that Co-Perpetrator Mother doing today? Did the child get help?

____

____

____

____

____

What would you say to the Co-Perpetrator Mother so she would understand that her child needs her to change?

____

____

____

____

____

SECTION II

CHANGE

CHAPTER 5

THE EDUCATED MOTHER UNDERSTANDING THE BATTLE

One way we can bring change is through understanding the battle we're in. Hence, the Educated Mother does her homework. She understands the battle by being informed. The Educated Mother learns to recognize the physical and emotional symptoms of sexual abuse for children of all ages and listens to her gut feelings. She follows through and talks to her child if she suspects that her child has been molested. This mother is smart and aware. Who is the Educated Mother?

SYMPTOMS OF SEXUAL ABUSE

The best way to fight the battle of child molestation is to learn the symptoms of sexual abuse. Several of these symptoms should be present in order to have reasonable suspicion that a child is being or has been molested. Different physical and emotional symptoms may manifest in children of different ages. Here are the symptoms to look for, broken down by age group.

Younger Children (Elementary Age Kids)

Physical

- Bedwetting - Regressive behavior
- Trouble sleeping
- Nightmares/bad dreams of monsters or being chased
- Withdrawing or being overly compliant
- Stomach pains
- Drawing unusual things
- Compulsive masturbation
- Wearing layers of clothes
- Seductive behaviors

Emotional

- Angry
- Tearful—crying for no reason
- Depressed
- Anxious
- Fearful

Teenagers (High School Age Teens)

Physical

- Trouble sleeping
- Nightmares
- Extreme behavioral changes

- Drastic changes in appearance—heavy makeup
- Substance Use—Alcohol and/or Drug Use
- Tardy for school and/or missing school
- Isolating—not participating in normal activities
- Changes in friendships
- Self-Mutilating—extreme body piercings
- Drawings/writings are dark and ugly in nature
- Sexually acting out
- Running away
- Pregnancy

Emotional

- Suicidal
- Depressed
- Anxious
- Fearful
- Changes in personality
- Low self-esteem

Sexual Signs for Children of All Ages

- Frequent urinary tract infections
- Rashes of itching in the private/genital area
- Symptoms of sexually transmitted infections, such as vaginal pain, unusual discharges, or sores in the private/ genital or oral areas
- Physical pain in the private/genital area

Following is one mother's story of how she followed her instincts after noticing her daughter's symptoms of sexual abuse.

KATE'S STORY

I knew something was wrong with my daughter when I noticed that she drastically changed. Kate's clothes changed from being light and playful to severely dark. She became more self-conscious and isolated. My daughter stopped doing her artwork, dancing, and singing. These activities were her passion. She had been fully alive but was now showing several signs of depression. I had to keep listening to my instincts in spite of the resistance I was getting from Kate. Over time with my persistence, her walls crumbled and the truth about her sexual abuse was finally revealed. I needed to be there for Kate before and after the secret came out.

HOW TO TALK TO CHILDREN ABOUT THEIR POSSIBLE SEXUAL ABUSE

If a mother notices several of the symptoms listed above, she can do many things to protect her child. First and foremost, DON'T PANIC! Take a deep breath and wait to gain your composure. Keep your anger and fear in check and remember you are mad and scared at the suspected perpetrator, not the child.

No specific time is right to ask the child questions because sexual abuse is a difficult topic. Nonetheless, start asking the child about what happened in privacy—not secrecy. Privacy is confidential, whereas secrecy implies that the abuse is too shameful to be revealed. Often the child will disclose what occurred willingly; it can be a huge relief for her. If the child is resistant, be patient and give the child time. Don't give up; keep asking questions.

After the child has disclosed the secret, BELIEVE the child no matter how shocking the story may seem. Kids don't make up sexual abuse. Thank the child for telling the secret. Tell her how brave she is to have told you what happened. Give her lots of verbal praise and emotional support. Most importantly, tell her, "It wasn't your fault." No child ever asks to be sexually abused. NEVER BLAME THE CHILD for what happened.

WHAT TO DO AFTER A CHILD DISCLOSES SEXUAL ABUSE

After the child discloses she has been sexually abused, get the child help. Take steps such as calling Child Protective Services to report what happened. They will let you know whether or not the police need to be called. Contact a child therapist who has been referred by your pediatrician or someone else you trust. Don't pressure the child to talk or to remain quiet about the sexual abuse. By allowing your child to talk about what happened when she is ready, she can have a sense of control over her life and the sexual abuse. Do not tell your child what to say about the sexual abuse. Let her use her own words.

Keep communication open with your child by asking her what she might need. If you aren't sure what to say or do, be truthful and tell the child but reassure her you will find out what to do and let her know when you have a better answer.

Never confront the suspected perpetrator in front of the child. Confrontation should only be handled by adults. The child does not need to be involved, and it will only cause her stress.

Continue to treat your child as a child. Don't use the abuse as an excuse to let her get out of her usual responsibilities. Remember she still has rules to follow, chores to complete, and school to attend. Continue to allow your child to play with friends and spend time in routine activities. Allow your child to express her feelings, whatever they may be. Be a good listener and try to set aside time regularly for "special talk time," when she can open her heart.

WHAT THE EDUCATED MOTHER CAN DO FOR HERSELF AFTER DISCLOSURE

When a child discloses sexual abuse to the Educated Mother, the mother will experience many feelings. She may even be tempted to kill the suspected perpetrator. However, this action is undesirable, since the child could lose the mother too. Other ways to fight back can bring more effective healing and change. The mother needs support. She needs someone she can talk and vent her emotions to. Major changes in the mother and child's life will now take place so having family and friends to help the Educated Mother through this trying, uncertain time is invaluable.

LISTEN TO YOUR GUT

As mothers, we have a sixth sense which detects when something is going on with our children. The mothers I interviewed talked repeatedly about "listening to my gut." If you don't notice many symptoms of sexual abuse, but your gut is telling you otherwise, investigate! If you start asking your child questions and aren't getting anywhere, but your intuition says more is going on, don't stop. Keep asking your child questions. If your suspicions are wrong, at least your child will know you are interested and attentive. One mother said, "I trust my intuition even though the situation might get messy."

SUMMARY

In understanding the battle, the Educated Mother brings change by knowing and looking for the symptoms of sexual abuse. She is not merely guessing something is wrong. She has a heightened sense of awareness because she is educated about the symptoms and warning signs. When she believes enough warning signs exist, she sets up a plan of action and talks to the child carefully, yet methodically. She listens to her gut even when the truth isn't revealed easily. She doesn't stop or get discouraged. She calls any authorities necessary to report suspected child sexual abuse. She is courageous as she marches into battle. In her innermost being is a love that far outweighs any darkness that tries to enter her home.

EXERCISE

What are two or three symptoms of sexual abuse you weren't aware of before reading this chapter?

____

____

____

____

If you were in this situation, what positive action might you take that would benefit you and your child after she has disclosed her sexual abuse?

____

____

____

____

____

Are you in touch with your intuition? Can you think of a time when you listened to your gut, even when the external facts didn't back up your suspicions? What happened? Was your intuition correct or incorrect?

____

____

____

____

____

CHAPTER 6

FACING THE ENEMY
PREPARING FOR THE BATTLE

The battle is fierce, and it is important to know the enemy we are fighting. This book would not be complete without information about perpetrators. While I do not pretend to be an expert in this field, I wish to provide some basic information to assist the Educated Mother in her mission to protect her child.

WHO ARE THE PERPETRATORS?

Perpetrators do not necessarily look different than anyone else. Most perpetrators are male, but women can molest children as well. Perpetrators come from all age groups. Some are not much older than their victims. Perpetrators can be of any race. They can be rich or poor which puts them in any socioeconomic class. They come from every type of community—city, suburbs, or rural areas. Their possible identities are endless.

WHERE AND WHEN DO PERPETRATORS MOLEST CHILDREN?

A child can be sexually abused anywhere and anytime. It can happen at home, at a friend's house, at a private or public school, at church, in a gym, at a sporting location, in a vehicle, in a city, and/or in the country. Molestation can happen in seconds. It can be happening while your child is unattended in the next isle at the toy store or playing a video game at an arcade. Molestation can happen during the day or night, before, during, or after school. Currently perpetrators are attracting children through cell phones and the internet via social media, chat rooms, and websites. Children are vulnerable. Therefore, parents need to be educated and aware and pass their education on to their young children.

HOW DO PERPETRATORS SEXUALLY ABUSE CHILDREN?

Statistics show that approximately 90 percent of perpetrators know their victims; therefore, it is rare for children to be molested by a stranger. Most perpetrators "groom" their victims intentionally or unconsciously. In other words, most children are slowly prepared for the abuse that is to follow.

Perpetrators typically groom children for abuse in one or more of the following ways:

1. **Controlling the child by using force or the power of authority.** Because the child is intimidated by the abuser, the child cooperates with the abuser's demands.

Commonly, a history of physical violence already exists in this situation, either between the child's parents, between the child and parent(s), or between the child and the abuser. The child sees no way to escape and from fear of greater personal harm, the child gives in to the perpetrator.

2. **Using gifts or "bribing" the child.** The abuser promises and gives special favors or items, such as toys, money, or personal attention to the child in exchange for doing what the perpetrator wishes. The child is "paid off" for his or her performance.

3. **Playing a "game" with the child.** The perpetrator introduces a "game" as a way to deceive the child into doing something sexually. For instance, the abuser may trick the child into playing a " fun touching game" which ends up being a sexual violation. This could include bouncing up and down on a perpetrator's lap, playing doctor and patient, or being asked to dance for the perpetrator.

4. **Confusing the child about the difference between love and sex.** The abuser grows closer to the child emotionally by spending time with the child. This might include babysitting the child while Mom goes shopping. The child and the perpetrator develop a "special" relationship which the adult uses to take advantage of the child's affection. This causes confusion for the child. The child often grows up

believing that they must perform sexually if they are to be loved.

A PERPETRATOR'S STORY

To bring further awareness to the public about molestation, I interviewed several men who were convicted of child sexual abuse. This particular case was about a grandfather who was repeatedly asked to watch his granddaughter while his wife and daughter went out to lunch and shopping. He soon became this child's regular babysitter and over time grew to be physically attracted to his granddaughter. He interpreted her innocent dancing and playing as seductive and inviting. Today, he realizes his selfishness and very much regrets his actions. Although his family has forgiven him, he is unable to forgive himself. Although he believes there may be a God, he feels too ashamed to consider God's forgiveness. This man agreed to be interviewed in hopes that his story will be heard by mothers who will learn from this example and become more educated to prevent a child from being sexually abused. This man's warning to mothers was to watch who cares for their children and be very cautious before agreeing to let a man do the childcare. If a man is too eager to watch the child, be suspicious. This perpetrator's opinion was that mothers trust too much and can be in denial about what may be happening to their children. He highly recommended that mothers always be very aware and pay attention to their children's words, behavior, and affections. According to him, it is best to ask children questions about their time spent with caregivers to ensure that nothing sexual has happened.

WHY DO PERPETRATORS SEXUALLY VIOLATE CHILDREN?

Perpetrators hurt children sexually for reasons that can be complex and vary from one person to another. Following are some of the more common reasons:

1. **The perpetrator was abused as a child.** Many perpetrators suffered some kind of abuse as a child, and the pattern of abuse is passed on from one generation to the next.

2. **The abuse may start as an impulse and then get out of control.** As in the perpetrator's story above, the abuse might begin simply as playfulness. It is not premeditated but impulsive and can quickly evolve into inappropriate sexual behavior.

3. **The perpetrator may be on a substance that breaks down inhibitions.** This includes prescription drugs, alcohol, and/or any mind-altering substances. It is very common that substances are involved when a

perpetrator crosses the line sexually with a child. The perpetrator's inhibitions are lessened by the substance resulting in poor judgement. Sometimes, the abuser may not even remember his actions.

4. **The perpetrator may have unresolved sexual issues or sexual frustration that, due to his other psychological problems, he tries to resolve by using the child.** For instance, because of his passive role he may be dominated and trapped in his adult relationship so he turns to a child sexually to gain a sense of power.

5. **The perpetrator may be addicted to child pornography.** Because of his psychological issues, he uses a child to reenact what he has seen in the pornography.

6. **The perpetrator may have unresolved issues about his sexual preference,** which in combination with other psychological problems leads him to use a same-sexed child to experiment or meet his sexual needs without having to risk being "ousted" in the adult world.

7. **The perpetrator has emotional problems.** The perpetrator may have emotional issues such as low self-esteem that make it difficult for him to get along with other adults. The perpetrator can better relate to a child. He then develops an inappropriate bond with the child which often times develops into sexual

contact. This would be evident when a teacher or a coach molests a student.

8. **The perpetrator feels a lack of control in his life.** He compensates for lack of self-esteem by using his power as an adult to build self-worth by controlling and molesting a vulnerable child.

Below is an interview with a perpetrator who had unresolved emotional problems and, as a result, crossed the line sexually with a child.

ANOTHER PERPETRATOR'S STORY

"It was the happiest time in my life," said this abuser. "My life was full of meaning and success." The perpetrator knew the family well. The families spent a lot of time together. The victim's father was working much of the time so was not able to give the child the affection that was necessary for a loving relationship. The mother would ask the perpetrator for parenting advice. He became a surrogate husband and dad to the family. He was gentle, compassionate, and listened to the child. He began developing attractions, feelings, and thoughts about the child. He became aware it was easier for him to bond with a child rather than an adult. The molestation occurred when he babysat this child for a weekend while the parents were out of town. The molest remained a secret for several months until the child told the parents about the incident. The perpetrator was arrested, charged, and found guilty. This perpetrator explained he continues to suffer every day from the awful crime he had committed and the bad decision that had lead him to do something so terrible to a child.

This perpetrator's advice to parents was to remember what is truly important in life, specifically, to take time to develop healthy relationships which require time and dedication. This life style helps to prevent molestation.

WAYS MOTHERS CAN SAFEGUARD AGAINST PERPETRATORS

Of the many perpetrators that were interviewed for this book, most had similar advice to mothers that would help safeguard their children from sexual abuse. The most prevalent statement was families need to get back to core values. They felt children would highly benefit from parents loving and respecting one another and spending quality time together as a family. They also recommended the parents develop a health relationship with their child by giving time, engaging with the child, and showing appropriate affection. If either parent has any emotional, psychological, or sexual hang-ups, they need to resolve them with a well-trained counselor. Both parents need to have healthy same sex friendships; however, because of the male tendency to isolate, it is crucial he have time with safe, stable men who he is accountable to for personal issues.

As a therapist who specializes in molestation, I teach mothers to role play possible situations that may arise in their child's life. This method teaches children how to say "No" to perpetrators and how to communicate that something "unusual" happened with someone. I use the "traffic light" analogy to teach young children and their parents the difference between good and bad touch or "go" and "stop". It is vital for the child's safety to keep clear communications. It is imperative for parents to integrate sex education and boundaries into their everyday parenting habits no matter the age of the child. A parent can start this practice when their child is an infant by watching for signs of molest. As their child becomes a toddler, parents can begin teaching them about good and bad touch. Consequently, education is the key for parents to safeguard their children from molestation.

SUMMARY

The Educated Mother learns about perpetrators' thoughts, actions, and manipulative tactics so she is aware of what is required to prevent her child from being molested. It is time to join the movement to protect our children to the best of our ability and to pass educational information on to all who will listen. It is through education that molestation is prevented. It is also through education and therapy that a family becomes equipped to break the cycle of generational molestation.

EXERCISE

What is one thing you learned about how perpetrators hurt children that you didn't know before?

____

____

____

____

____

What might you say to or do with your child to "safe proof" him or her against an abuser?

____

____

____

____

____

What is something you have learned that you will share with another mother to help her protect her child from perpetrators?

____

____

____

____

____

CHAPTER 7

BLOWING UP BELIEFS
REVISING BATTLE TACTICS

Many beliefs exist that an Educated Mother of molested children must contend with in order to protect her child and bring change. Let's take a close look at these beliefs to learn from them and separate which are myths and which have some validity.

BELIEF # 1: THE MOTHER OF A MOLESTED CHILD SHOULD KNOW ABOUT THE ABUSE

The most common belief about child sexual abuse is that the mother should know about the abuse. Mothers commonly blame themselves for the abuse saying, "I should have known my child was being molested." Perpetrators can be either so calculating or so impulsive that their behavior is difficult to predict. Most perpetrators are masters at deceiving others and covering their tracks. They are like hunters covering the traps for their prey. Other perpetrators may not even know what they are going to do until the opportunity arises. Hence, mothers of molestation survivors should not automatically blame themselves when sexual abuse occurs. The educated mother is better equipped to initially recognize the warning signs of molestation and prevent further harm.

The action a mother takes after the molestation is exposed is most important to the child's recovery and healing process. The important question is not, "Did the mother know about the sexual abuse?" but, "What did she do when she learned about the abuse?" Hopefully, MOMS will stop the sexual abuse as soon as it is exposed.

BELIEF #2: AUTHORITIES ALWAYS DO THEIR JOBS EFFECTIVELY

In most cases, authorities such as Child Protective Services, Police/Sheriffs, and Family Law, Criminal or Civil Court officers work very hard to bring the truth to light and ensure justice is served. Each of these systems has heavy responsibilities, and staff members are often overwhelmed by the demands of their jobs. They may have too few resources to thoroughly handle all the cases they receive. In addition, it can be difficult for the authorities to pinpoint incontrovertible evidence to support accusations of molestation, no matter how sympathetic they may be to the child and mother.

It is imperative that a mother do her best to represent her child in these systems. She needs to be assertive and stand up for her child and herself. Below is the story of a mother who courageously did so.

CHARLOTTE'S STORY

I married my second husband when my daughter was eight years old. Marriage problems began when I became pregnant a couple of years later. Problems between us became worse and I sensed he was having an affair with someone because of his detached and secretive demeanor. Shortly after our son was born I learned he was not having an affair. Rather my husband was molesting his stepdaughter.

One day at school, as my daughter watched a video on sex education it became clear to her that she had been raped by her stepfather. She told a friend who in turn told the teacher. The teacher called the police who came to school to talk to my daughter. They sent her home alone where her stepfather was waiting for her. It was not until this time that I received a phone call from the school counselor informing me of the situation.

As I confronted my husband and he confessed to this crime, I listened in disbelief. I was raised to believe that a stranger would harm a child not a family member. In shame, my husband left the house immediately. However, the police did not contact me for another two days at which time they informed me I may be losing my daughter because

I had failed to protect her. Shortly after, I received a summons from the court stating I was being charged with being an unfit mother. At court the judge authorized a forensic psychologist to evaluate the case and he eventually determined I was a fit mother worthy of continuing to raise my daughter.

Although my husband had two felonies, he was not sentenced to jail time. Rather, he received three years of psychological treatment. Our family tried to reconcile but it failed, because he lied constantly about his progress. If I had to do it over again, I would do anything necessary to make sure he served jail time. He showed no remorse and acted as though his crime was not serious.

BELIEF # 3: TEENAGE GIRLS LEARN ABOUT THEIR SEXUALITY FROM THEIR PARENTS

Unfortunately, teenage girls (and boys) often learn about their sexuality by dating, clubbing, partying, getting advice from their peers, social media and/or reading literature such as magazine articles oriented toward teenagers. Consequently, they are often unprepared for what lies ahead. However, it is a myth these are the only avenues teens use to learn about their sexuality. A teenage girl needs an adult woman to talk to, preferably her mother, an aunt, or a trusted family friend.

Teenage girls should be taught how to avoid dangerous situations. Mothers need to discuss safety with their daughters to help prevent sexual abuse from occurring. Here are some simple safety rules every teenager should know:

1. When young ladies go to a bar, club, or party together, they should leave together. No matter how nice the male appears or how well she knows him, she should not leave with him.

2. If she and her friends will be drinking alcohol, they should have a designated driver who will NOT drink and who will drive them home.

3. Similarly, if they are drinking, they should never leave their drinks unattended to prevent anyone from slipping Rohypnol, GHB, or any other sedative into their drinks.

4. Her cell phone should be pre-programmed with the local police dispatch number in case of emergency. Pre-programming the number for an Uber or a taxicab company into her cell phone is also a good idea in case the designated driver decides to drink and shouldn't drive.

5. Another good precaution is to give her a credit card with limited credit available to use in this crisis situation.

6. A rule some parents have is no matter the time of day or night, they will pick their children up from

anywhere, no questions asked—until the next day—even if their children are drunk or high. The next day, they will talk. (This does not mean that these parents promote getting drunk or high. They are realistic, and the most important issue is their children escape potentially dangerous situations).

Again, parents should discuss these safety rules with their teenagers and put them into action. Prevention will not ward off all perpetrators, but it is the best way to protect your teenager.

BELIEF # 4: ONLY GIRLS ARE VICTIMS OF SEXUAL ABUSE

Another belief is sexual abuse only happens to girls. THAT IS NOT TRUE. I provide individual and group counseling for male survivors who were molested by male and female perpetrators. There aren't as many individual or group counseling services or as much literature available for male survivors, but these resources do exist. Although many similarities exist in the forms of treatment for sexually abused males and females, some differences need to be addressed in treatment. For instance, if the male victim's perpetrator is female, the male victim often has issues dealing with his masculinity, becoming either overly passive or overly aggressive towards women. Hopefully, there will be further research on the problems and treatment, and thus more information on ways to overcome male sexual abuse in the future. For now, remember males are victims of sexual abuse too, and mothers need to protect them as well!

BELIEF # 5: ONLY STRANGERS ARE PERPETRATORS

Many people believe that only "strangers" molest children. However, as the stories so far demonstrate, perpetrators are often people close to their victims. That said it is important to educate children to be wary of strangers and to be properly educated about the warning signs of a perpetrator looking for a victim.

Following is the story of one girl's encounter with a potential perpetrator that would not have happened had she been educated about such behavior.

KAREN'S STORY

I was twelve, and I babysat two children in a large city while their mother was at work. We would go to the park. One day, there was a man in the park who asked for permission to photograph me. He asked me to pose with my chest out although at the age of twelve, I was flat-chested and skinny. At first, I didn't understand what was happening but soon realized something was wrong and very inappropriate. When this stranger put his hand in my shirt to "lift my breasts up" I became alarmed and immediately took the children and left the park. I never told anyone about this incident.

In this story, the potential perpetrator tried to entice Karen by beginning with an activity that was seemingly innocent. Fortunately, Karen was smart enough to leave (and was in a situation where she was able to do so) before she could be further abused. It's important to note that even though Karen was in a public place with other children, she was still not safe from a perpetrator.

86

SUMMARY

Many beliefs about molestation need to be understood in more detail to bring about prevention, change, and healing. The Educated Mother learns about these beliefs and the realities behind them to prevent abuse from happening in the first place and to bring healing if a child has been harmed. There is power in knowing the facts about molestation.

EXERCISE

Has your understanding changed about any of the beliefs mentioned above?

____

____

____

____

____

What "safety rules" might you adopt for your teenager about dating or partying with friends?

____

____

____

____

____

Do you ask your children about the people they meet during the day? Do you ask details about their encounters with strangers? Are they willing to share this information with you?

____

____

____

____

____

SECTION III

HEALING

CHAPTER 8

THE RESOURCEFUL MOTHER HEALING FROM THE BATTLE

THE NEED FOR IMMEDIATE INDIVIDUAL COUNSELING

Once the Resourceful Mother realizes that her child has been molested, she gets help for her child so the healing process can begin. Immediately, this mother finds a good child therapist who does art and play therapy to start treatment for her young child's sexual abuse.

Different avenues exist for finding a child therapist. One way is to contact your pediatrician for a referral. Most medical doctors have therapists they recommend. Another method is to contact your health insurance company. Find the 800 phone number on your healthcare card to telephone your provider or go online to view the child therapists in your area. Your healthcare provider will give you a list of mental health providers who specialize in working with children in your area. You might also seek out family community agencies that provide counseling for children and offer lower-income families a sliding scale for payment. Contacting your church for resources can be another means of finding an experienced child therapist. A personal referral is usually one of the best ways to get a good recommendation for a child counselor.

In some circumstances, it may be best to find a "forensic" therapist. This type of therapist specializes in working with the court system, specifically cases that involve child sexual assault. A forensic therapist is able to evaluate a child, provide treatment, and testify in court if necessary. The local court will usually recognize the forensic therapist's abilities and allow his or her opinion in the court system. It is best to consider this avenue when there is an extremely high-conflict situation. Most family law attorneys can recommend well-respected child/family therapists.

When interviewing a therapist for your child, start by having at least one session alone with the therapist before treatment begins. It is important for the therapist to obtain a significant family history, the details of the circumstances that bring you to seek counseling for your child, and your main concerns and goals for treatment. Depending on the child's age, the therapist may be limited in what he or she will share with the parent due to confidentiality issues; teenagers generally need more privacy in therapy than younger children in order to heal fully. However, it is a good idea for parents to get updates regarding treatment as appropriate and available. Some courts will allow the child therapist to communicate regarding the child's treatment; however, this situation can be very uncertain due to the family court system's complexities. Consequently, MOMS should seek legal advice before the therapist communicates with the courts.

FAMILY COUNSELING IS ALSO NECESSARY

In addition to individual therapy for the child, family therapy is also important and should be started as soon as possible. Depending on the situation, the mother, father or boyfriend, and siblings may also need a professional to talk to regarding the situation. It is also often beneficial to have a few sessions where everyone can discuss the event(s). Some agencies specialize in treating families who have experienced sexual abuse. These agencies provide counseling for the victim, siblings, and parents. If the perpetrator is a family member, the agency may provide counseling for him as well. The family can self-refer, receive a referral, or be directed by court order to a local agency that treats the entire family.

When the father is the perpetrator, the mother is referred to in official documents and reports as "the non-offending parent." This term often seems inadequate to describe an innocent mother who faces terrible trauma. I believe the mother is a survivor just like the child is which is why I've coined the term "Mothers of Molestation Survivors."

INDIVIDUAL THERAPY IS
RECOMMENDED FOR THE MOTHER

Most of the mothers I interviewed said nothing had ever been more devastating for them than learning their children were sexually abused. With rare exceptions, mothers have an innate instinct to protect and love their children. This drive can lead them to perform superhuman deeds to protect their children, such as lifting heavy objects off their child which they would never attempt under normal circumstances.

But fully protecting one's child requires more than feats of strength. The Resourceful Mother who wishes to protect her child will start individual counseling so she can take care of her own recovery, thereby making her strong enough to battle for her child. The circumstances are too traumatizing for her to contend with alone.

MOTHERS ARE USUALLY TREATED FOR POST-TRAUMATIC STRESS DISORDER

The typical diagnosis MOMS are given is Post-Traumatic Stress Disorder (PTSD). Unfortunately, mothers may be misdiagnosed with anxiety or depression, thus delaying their full recovery until they are diagnosed and treated for PTSD. It is also usual for a mother to be diagnosed with depression in addition to PTSD, in which case an anti-depressant medication can be helpful.

PTSD symptoms result after a person has experienced a life-threatening incident or serious injury that creates intense feelings of fear, horror, or helplessness. This results in flashbacks or recurrent distressing dreams or thoughts of the event which trigger feelings of hyper-vigilance, detachment, anger, and renewed feelings of intense fear, horror, or helplessness. Difficulty sleeping or concentrating, diminished interest in everyday responsibilities, and avoidance of anything related to the trauma are also common symptoms. It is important to note that while the mother did not herself experience the sexual trauma, she often undergoes the same fears and trauma as if she *had* experienced the event.

Traditional talk therapy is helpful and often used to treat PTSD. Another useful treatment modality is Eye Movement Desensitization and Reprocessing (EMDR)[1]. It is a neurologically-based treatment that is very effective because it is short-term and less intrusive than some other therapies. EMDR was invented by Dr. Frances Shapiro in the late 1980's. This method basically works by restoring brain activity through manipulating eye movement.

Trauma causes part of the brain to slow down and that part of the brain to function improperly. EMDR causes a person's eyes to move back and forth helping the same part of the brain reactivates and become desensitized to the memory. A specialized therapist will use a particular protocol to help the brain reprocess the memory. When people are traumatized, they will first try to fight the situation. If they are unable to fight, they will try to flee. When they can't fight or flee, they will freeze. Freezing is a primitive instinct that we all possess. By freezing, our hope is to stay alive and somehow escape the harm brought upon us. Our brains more or less stay in this "frozen state" after the trauma. This is why people with PTSD relive their trauma over and over again: a part of the brain called the hypothalamus is literally stuck in the trauma.

There was a time in my personal life I experienced PTSD. When I learned about EMDR in a continuing education class on trauma, I was doubtful this type of treatment would be effective but had been unsuccessful up to this point in finding relief from my trauma. After receiving EMDR from a specialized therapist in my community, my life changed for the better and my skepticism about this treatment method vanished[2]. As a result of my personal experience, I earned a special certification in EMDR enabling me to provide this treatment to my clients. In my private practice, I use EMDR with nearly 80 percent of the clients I treat. I believe the counseling field is changing to include more extensive research on the effects of psychological trauma and the brain.

OTHER ISSUES A RESOURCEFUL MOTHER MAY WANT TO WORK THROUGH IN COUNSELING

Mothers of molestation survivors will also benefit from counseling in other areas.

If a mother whose child was molested was abused herself as a child, this is a good opportunity for her to deal with her own sexual abuse, if she hasn't done so already. It is never too late to work through past issues to enable healing. When I began my career as an intern, one of the first patients I treated was seventy-six years old! I'll never forget how brave she was to do psychotherapy.

It is not uncommon for the mother of a molestation survivor to wonder whether her child was molested because she did not meet her husband/boyfriend's sexual needs. Mothers may ask themselves, "Why would he choose to have sex with my child instead of me?" Just as in rape or sexual assault of adults, CHILD SEXUAL ABUSE IS NOT ABOUT SEX. It is important for mothers to remember that perpetrators cross the line for many reasons, as stated in Chapter 6[1].

Another issue a mother often faces after she learns her child has been molested by her partner is low self-esteem. This causes her to question her sexuality and sensuality, without counseling, she may seek validation through casual sexual encounters or relationships. Through counseling she can discover strength from within and not need validation from a sexual partner.

"RAGE, RAGE, RAGE! All I could see was RED!" said one mother of a molested child. A mother in this situation has a lot to be angry about, such as having trusted a man she loved to care for her child, only to have him betray her trust. Anger can arise from the disclosure of the secret and the consequences including legal ramifications, financial crises, and family changes. MOMS feel "righteous anger" in these situations. It is necessary and healthy for MOMS to be angry so they can express themselves and process the situation in a safe place with a counselor.

Grief is part of the rage felt by the mother of a molested child. She is forced into what may feel like a death. The mother may grieve for the loss of all that she thought she had—her mate, her sense of safety, and the definition of herself as a good mother because she was not able to protect her child. In the end, she needs to rebuild her life which will require all of her strength and courage. Overcoming the incredible trauma and moving forward in a positive fashion takes an amazingly committed woman.

---

1. For more information on EMDR, visit www.EMDR.com

2. To find an EMDR therapist, visit www.EMDRIA.org and click on "Find A Therapist."

SUMMARY

The Resourceful Mother of a molested child is one of the most courageous women imaginable. The process of healing and recovery is hard work; but the healthy, resourceful mother doesn't stop until she and her family find some semblance of healing. Eventually, she may think the work is done only to have the wounds reopen a year or two later when unexpected issues surrounding the topic arise. Dan Allender, author of The Wounded Heart, wrote of sexual abuse, "It is not over until you die." Unfortunately, this comment is very true. The Resourceful Mother is aware of the need for ongoing treatment because the past cannot be erased. However, it can be healed so she and her family can live life in a productive, peaceful manner.

EXERCISE

If needed, would you be willing to attend counseling to help yourself and your family? Why or why not?

____

____

____

____

Have you heard of EMDR prior to reading this book? What is your opinion of EMDR? Would you be willing to try it?

____

____

____

____

Is there any information about the resourceful mother that was unfamiliar to you?

____

____

____

____

CHAPTER 9

PRACTICAL WAYS TO BRING HEALING

The Resourceful Mother diversifies and finds other methods beyond professional counseling and therapy to bring healing to her child, family, and herself. She realizes she and her family members have been wounded on many different levels which require finding sources of healing that fit the individual. The following ideas are focused on personal methods MOMS might use for herself or use to help family members and friends.

FINDING PEACE

In the middle of any battle, one can benefit from gaining some form of peace. One mother I counseled found a personal source of healing by helping others in need who had suffered from a similar trauma. Taking the focus from her tragedy and placing the focus elsewhere brought her a sense of self-worth by showing kindness to others. The Resourceful Mother can bring healing by learning to "be mindful". I define it as teaching oneself to come back into her body, mind, and spirit by coming back to the present "moment". It is as simple as asking oneself, "What do you see, hear, feel, taste, touch, and smell?"

Experiencing theses senses automatically brings a person back to a peaceful moment.

Coming back to the moment exercise is not used only for trauma but can be used daily. We seem to be in such a hurry these days that allowing ourselves to be centered is helpful. I like to do this exercise with my children. We will have a "moment" while we are driving around town on a busy afternoon which is very calming. It is also helpful to incorporate deep breathing into this exercise. Taking deep breaths and slowly exhaling three times in a row relaxes a person.

Sitting in silence is another way to find peace. Although most mothers have a family life filled with disruptions, their day may seem more peaceful when they find time to sit quietly by themselves. Perhaps time could be set aside before the day's activities begin or when the children have gone to bed. Some people find slowly rocking back and forth to be soothing while sitting quietly. The rocking motion is neurologically calming, which is why babies like to be rocked and the elderly like to sit in rocking chairs.

REST, REST, AND MORE REST

Research has shown that most people persevere through a crisis only to find them physically ill after the crisis is over. When a person is in crisis, her adrenal glands kick in and provide the stamina she needs to perform. However, particularly with long-term stress, the adrenal glands get depleted, and the person will physically crash. This crash may include autoimmune deficiencies. In order to prevent a physical crash, it is strongly recommended that the Resourceful Mother, whose child has been sexually abused, make time to rest. A perfect time to nap is while your child is napping. Learn to take fifteen-minute "power naps." If you are not able to sleep because of children who need supervision, lay or sit down and rest while watching them. Until you have recovered physically from the crisis, periodically find one twenty-four hour period to rest while someone trusted watches your children.

One mother I interviewed found a monastery through the Catholic Church where she could go for a personal retreat. It was very inexpensive, and it was quiet because there were no televisions, radios, or other electronics. It was the perfect place for quiet reflection and rest. A local hotel or a friend's home can serve as a retreat as well.

SELF-CARE

A mother is inclined to forget about her well-being when she is focused on her suffering child. If this lack of personnel care persists, the mother will be unable to care for her child. Taking care of her insures that she will be physically and emotionally able to tackle any future problems that may arise for herself or her child. Self-care for a mother includes not only eating healthy and going for routine medical exams but making time to pamper herself.

Here are some examples of self-care:

- Resting
- Eating right
- Taking vitamins
- Exercising: take a short walk or get an exercise tape that you can use at home
- Getting an annual medical exam, including a breast and gynecological exam
- Taking a bubble bath
- Drinking a hot cup of tea
- Reading a mindless magazine or novel
- Taking time to spend with close girlfriends
- Taking time to enjoy a hobby such as gardening or photography. Your children can participate in both of these hobbies with you. Their little hands are great for pulling small weeds or planting tiny seeds. Your children are always wonderful subjects for your photography.

One mother I interviewed told me one day she decided she would read a novel that was easy to read and effortless. When her daughter saw her mother reading, she said, "I didn't know you could read." At first, this comment may seem funny, but it says it all. Take care of yourself; you are irreplaceable to your child.

BUILD YOUR SUPPORT SYSTEM

As previously mentioned, when friends or family members hear about child sexual abuse, they tend to take sides. Therefore, it is not uncommon for MOMS to lose people who have supported them in the past. Consequently, MOMS are forced to build new friendships. It is important to remember that this process takes time. Other places to build new friendships might be through a mother's group in the community or at church. You might also try reconnecting with old friends you haven't seen in a while. Sometimes older women who have lived through hardships can be a wonderful, positive support and offer their personal stories as testimonies of personal perseverance.

One mother I interviewed made an important point. She regretted dating too early in her recovery process. Looking back, she realized that time spent working on her personal issues would have better prepared her for a healthy, successful relationship with a male support system. When a mother decides to delay dating while resolving her trauma, she significantly decreases her chances of repeating any negative patterns in her relationships with men.

SUMMARY

Mothers of Molestation Survivors can bring healing into their lives by using the resources all around them. Notably, most of these resources are small things that can be easily incorporated into a mother's life. It is step by step and moment by moment that change and healing occur. It maybe through the simple things, like enjoying a beautiful daisy or the scent of a lavender candle, that we can find pleasure once again. The Resourceful Mother may also be healed and transformed through planning self-care. Ultimately, one of the greatest restorations for a mother is to hear the sound of her child's laughter especially when that laughter has been quieted for a long period of time.

EXERCISE

Can you list additional ways other than those listed above that might help a woman take care of herself?

____

____

____

____

In what way you are willing to try to take care of yourself this week?

____

____

____

____

How might reconnecting with your spiritual side or building a relationship with God help you through your recovery? Who is in your support system? How can you improve on it?

____

____

____

____

SECTION IV

TRANSFORMATION

CHAPTER 10

THE SPIRITUAL MOTHER
THE BATTLE IS BIGGER THAN US

If you have made it this far in this book, my hope is that you will hear me out in this chapter as well. My interviews indicated some mothers who had a spiritual belief in God or a Higher Power or a religious orientation were able to contend with difficult questions related to their belief. However, other mothers were in the process of losing her faith, which caused feelings of grief, confusion, loss and bitterness, especially if a religious member of a congregation was involved in the sexual abuse. There were, of course, other mothers that were non-religious and found similar comfort in other ways. Lastly, mothers who were non-religious were upset or irritated when someone tried to provide spiritual comfort. Thus, there are many walks of life, and to address one orientation to life of spirituality may benefit someone. In fact, I would now like to share some of the spiritual lessons the MOMS I interviewed shared with me in hopes that their stories will benefit you as well.

SPIRITUAL LESSONS
THAT BROUGHT MOMS TRANSFORMATION

I will never forget one Spiritual Mother who shared with me the story of her child's sexual abuse and how she later became transformed. When this mother spoke to a Catholic priest, he told her that child sexual abuse is not what God would ever want for her child or any other child. It was not God's will for this abuse to happen. God was heartbroken and He was aware of her tears over this devastation with her. This mother felt that this viewpoint was a new and refreshing way to see God. I agree with her and the priest that God would not want any child to be harmed in this manner; God does hear our cries.

Similarly, another therapist and I were talking one time about how there may be a special place in Hell for unrepentant perpetrators. Our concept of Hell was endless talking, crying, and NOISE. The idea of perpetrators having to listen eternally to noise, including their victim's cries and screams from the harm they caused, sounded like some justice.

It is in our best interest to understand vengeance is not our responsibility. Of course, most MOMS are tempted and dream of vengeance, but the "vengeance" that perpetrators face is worse than we can ever imagine. Furthermore, I have to believe that most perpetrators create their own prisons here on earth, especially if they haven't suffered legally for their actions. The perpetrator's prison is his mind. Those perpetrators that are remorseful, replay what he did to the child over and over, trying to forget it or change it in some way —but the deed can never be erased.

When a perpetrator takes away a child's innocence for his own gratification, such selfishness is the very core of evil. No justification can exist for this behavior. Some people use free will in a bad way, and will be accountable to God for misusing the gift He gave us. God sees it all; He knows.

One Spiritual Mother I interviewed shared the only way she could cope with the knowledge of her child's abuse was to surrender the battle to God. She realized the battle was bigger than her. She also believed that God is big enough to use the sexual abuse in her daughter's life at some time in the future for good. She commented that perhaps her daughter would help other children who had suffered from such abuse. This mother also believed God could use this tragedy in her child's life to build her character. She shared with me the following Bible verse: "God can use all things for his good according to those who are called by Christ Jesus" (Romans 8:28, NIV Version). When I interviewed people from other religions or even non-religious individuals, they were aware children need lessons to develop and individuate. Child sexual abuse can provide this opportunity for a child, as we never know how a child can use their experience to benefit society someday.

Similarly, another Spiritual Mother was transformed when she shared from her heart that she had finally realized her child is not her own. She learned her child is a gift given to her by God to nurture, shape, and prepare to grow into a mature adult. It is a novel thought to consider that our children are gifts from God. We only have the opportunity to mold, change, and love our children until age eighteen. We forget that they are not ours, but we do have the opportunity and privilege to be part of their lives. This revelation assisted this MOM to look at the situation in a broader perspective and understand her child can grow from this horrible situation.

The Bible talks about how sins are passed down from one generation to another. MOMS break this generational cycle when they protect their children and stop the abuse. When the mother of a molestation survivor takes action, spiritual things occur, whether the mother is aware of it or not. When a mother acts, she is saying, "Enough is enough; no more sexual abuse in this family line!"

The Spiritual Mothers I interviewed found great comfort and help in prayer. They expressed how God had answered their prayers by bringing people from the church to provide emotional support and even assist them with legal issues in these times of darkness and transformation. They saw child molestation as a spiritual battle between good and evil, right and wrong, God and Satan. Through their own and others' prayers, these MOMS gained strength, insight, and hope that good would prevail. Since not all religions and/or non-religious persons believe in good and bad, they saw the battle through a different spiritual lens, such as how their child could benefit from their traumatic experience in time or down the road.

Many of the Spiritual Mothers told me their faith was tested during this battle. They agonized over the devastation that occurred. They cried out to God; at times, they screamed at Him in anger, knowing He was big enough to hear them and understand. A mother was comforted by a verse in the Bible found in Lamentations 3:58-60, "Lord, you took up my case; you redeemed my life. You have seen, O Lord, the wrong done to me. Uphold my cause!" Another mother shared a vision she had of being rewarded for her suffering in the battle of her child's sexual abuse. This vision allowed her to continue the battle: she now felt that she knew her efforts were not in vain, because God supported her in her fight for her child.

Most of the women I interviewed shared they grew closer to God and developed stronger spiritual lives. It is common for us to look beyond ourselves when we are in such deep pain. We start to ask ourselves tough questions, like, "Where is God in this madness?" There are no quick or easy answers to such questions. I can report, however, that many MOMS found comfort in a new, revitalized relationship with God as they went through this traumatic situation. One mother explained she found God to be her "safe place," and He consoled her and healed her pain. Other non-religious MOMS had similar questions to the universe they yelled out. In time, they too were able to find a release in asking these tough questions.

SUMMARY

Spiritual Mothers are strong. They have fought the battle of child sexual abuse on a deep level in their spirits. They have struggled with hard questions, pain too deep to express, and they have come out on the other side with a stronger belief in God. Other MOMS who were non-religious found comfort in other ways through insightful friends, inspiring poems and/or encouraging music. Most bookstores carry small devotional books in many different denominations, which provide short, inspirational daily readings. These readings are a great quick way to start your day by reconnecting with your spirit and reshaping how you understand life as you continue to heal from the pain. These Spiritual MOMS are unlike others. Who can know them?

EXERCISE

How do you see God or a Higher Power in your child's trauma?

____

____

____

____

If you are non-religious, what have you found to give you comfort in the darkest moments of your situation?

____

____

____

____

Whether you are religious or not, how might you see your child learn, develop and/or use this horrible experience in their life?

____

____

____

____

ADVICE FOR THE BATTLE

The following compiled advice and knowledge was shared by many of the mothers who through their hearts, minds, and souls wanted to support other MOMS who may find themselves in similar situations. This information is also invaluable for fathers, families, caregivers, and friends who wish to understand the detrimental situation. Understanding would enable them to be better equipped to provide support and encouragement. It is based on knowledge gained in a spiritual manner through the hearts, minds, souls, and guts of mothers. I have gathered this advice from MOMS to provide further support, encouragement, and hope to other MOMS and those seeking to help them,

LISTEN TO YOUR CHILD

First and foremost, listen to your child. Even though you are overwhelmed and consumed with daily living, nothing is more important than making time each day to check in with your child. Lie down with your child at night and find out how she is, how her day went, what she did, and what she didn't like about the day. Then, wait patiently for a response. You may be surprised what your child is willing to share when they have your focused attention. If the need is there, continue asking questions. We need to enter into the child's world rather than expect the child to enter into ours.

I have found when counseling parents of teenagers that their teenager is expected to "listen to them." However, during the teenage years, a shift occurs where teens need to have the rules clarified rather than when they were younger and simply followed them. When a parent is able to discuss and negotiate the rules with them as they enter their teen years, the parent-child relationship is smoother. Also attempt to understand your children by reading their magazines, playing their video games, going to their movies, and listening to their music. Remember, the teenager's world is an entirely different world from yours. Finally, remember that if a parent becomes a "lecturer," the parent will often lose the teenager's attention which causes a power struggle that defeats your goal of communicating effectively with your child.

REMEMBER THE BASIC FAMILY RULES

Remember the basic "rules" of a healthy family. First, make sure you are providing the basic issues your children require such as physical and emotional needs. Besides providing food and shelter, ask your children regularly how they are doing emotionally. Keep communications open with them. Most importantly, keep your promises to your child. This allows them to build trust in relationships and creates a sense of security.

Additionally, face conflict in the family as it arises. Teach your children problem solving techniques. There may be more conflict after the secret of child sexual abuse is revealed, but the best approach is to deal with it immediately. These basic guidelines assist a family in functioning in a healthy manner.

Another emotional needs a child may have is in situations where a male adult in the household is the perpetrator, often the child may be angry that the father/boyfriend is no longer in the home. Sometimes the child displaces her anger at the mother and acts out accordingly. The child doesn't understand all that has happened and is hurting. You may find it difficult to reason with your child when she displaces her anger at you, so it is best to bring this matter to the child's therapist.

BOUNDARIES ARE IMPORTANT

Another important factor in fighting the battle is personal boundaries. It is appropriate for the parent to refrain from using their child as a confidante to whom they unload and process their personal emotions. Remember what responsibilities you have as a parent in this regard and perhaps your child might need to be reminded of their role in this process as well. Adults and children have separate needs and desires that need to be addressed. When someone's boundaries have been dishonored, it is important to ask questions to get more information and take action

TALK ABOUT THE SUBJECT

The MOMS I interviewed recommended molestation should no longer be kept a secret. Rather, try to educate the person you will be sharing this secret with to help them understand the great need to be supportive not only to you individually but to anyone in this situation. Because talking about molestation is taboo in today's society, millions of secrets are held in silence. However, little by little, brave survivors have been publically sharing their stories. When a mom shares her story she must tell people who are trustworthy. Asking a friend just to walk through the process with her is an excellent way for her to have someone to express herself to during this difficult experience. For example, one mother mentioned it was helpful when a close friend went to family court with her.

Use wisdom when talking to people about these circumstances. Sometimes it is important *not* to listen to everyone because some people may not have the right information. Therefore, if you think the information will harm you or your child, discard it.

GET BACK ON YOUR FEET

Although it is a trying time in many ways for a mother who learns that her child has been molested, it is necessary for her to get back on her feet. Mothers I interviewed were very candid about the realities of what lay ahead for them. They needed to restore some sense of normalcy in the home, find a job, develop support, and get back into daily living. But most importantly, a mother needs to gain back her confidence in herself and her abilities as a mother and woman. She needs to be strong and assertive.

REASSURE THE MOTHER OF A MOLESTATION SURVIVOR

Like the child who has experienced sexual abuse, the mother also needs to hear repeatedly, "It wasn't your fault. You are not to blame." This reassurance may be found through family and friends. Although mothers have wonderful intuition and may be trained to look for signs of sexual abuse, sometimes it is impossible for MOMS to know that their children are being hurt, especially if their children have been convinced by the perpetrators not to share their secrets. Again, it is what a mother does after she learns of the abuse that is most significant. Remember "You did the best you could under the circumstances."

HOPE OF A SAFER WORLD

According to Maslow's Hierarchy of Needs, human's greatest needs are food, shelter, safety and security, and ultimately belonging and being loved. When America was attacked on September 11, 2001, I believe what shocked most Americans was until that day, they believed the United States was invincible and we as Americans were safe from a devastating attack. In the weeks and months that followed, I noticed a change in my client's attitudes and presenting issues. They exhibited new levels of anxiety that I had not observed before. I concluded that the anxiety level was greater because people were affected to the core of their beings when they realized we, as a nation, were vulnerable. I realized that children who had been molested must feel this same sense of insecurity when their world is violated.

As the world watched on September 11 while New York City's finest landmarks collapsed in heaps of rubble, the instant outpouring of sacrificing one's life for that of a stranger showed humanity in their greatest form. Similarly, the world that children live in today is collapsing while molestation claims the security of the family unit. Humanity needs to meet the greatest form of selflessness by creating a world that is safe for our children by working together to break the cycle of generational molestation.

SUMMARY

Mothers of molestation survivors have a great deal of advice for other mothers. These mothers who were interviewed provided insight into effective ways to communicate and make themselves, their children, and their families stronger in order to get through the battle. We can learn from their wisdom. By implementing this advice, transformation of families, communities, and the world will occur.

EXERCISE

What is one thing that you learned that these MOMS provided?

____

____

____

____

____

What is one way you will communicate differently with your child?

____

____

____

____

____

Now that you have this valuable advice, what are you going to do with it?

____

____

____

____

____

CHAPTER 12

SPEAKING AFTER THE BATTLE

When the mother of a molestation survivor begins to come out of the battle, it is human nature to want to forget about hurtful events. She commonly wants to move on and leave the terrible experience behind. The time comes when her child and other family members are functioning better, the legal issues are nearly resolved, and she is recovering from financial losses. When some sense of ordinary life is reinstated, it is common for the mother to not want to continue to talk about the event. Even when some good things come out of these difficult situations, such as being a stronger mother and woman, most MOMS just want to forget the whole experience. This feeling is understandable. But mothers of molestation survivors need to unite and find a voice.

MOMS Must Unite and Share Their Stories
There is Power in Standing Together

As with anything in life, we feel empowered when we are supported by one another for a common goal. Can you imagine the impact of MOMS uniting and sharing their vision of a world free of child sexual abuse? Change will occur when people begin to speak more freely about the subject of molestation and find the courage to share their stories. Sharing your story will encourage other MOMS and families who are going through a similar situation. Through your story, mothers and families can perhaps avoid some of the pain and hardship by learning lessons you have to share. As educational material is accepted and learned, families and communities will become stronger enabling children to get help faster which will help in the recovery process. As families accept the responsibility to educate their preschool age children about age appropriate sexual topics, and parents learn about sexual development in children, how to properly educate their children about sexual issues, symptoms of child sexual abuse, safety rules, and what to do if their child discloses sexual abuse, the incidents of molestation will begin to decline.

Using this book as educational material and sharing the information with all who will listen, is an important step. Join MOMS as we unite in "supporting moms to make a difference in their children's lives".

Won't you please join me in this effort to unite these MOMS? If you are a mother whose child was sexually abused and you want to tell your story, or you need information or resources, please contact me. Pass this book and information on to other mothers. Speak up. Use your voice. It's time to UNITE NOW!

EXERCISE

Why is it crucial for MOMS to share their stories?

____

____

____

____

How can change occur when MOMS share their stories?

____

____

____

____

What have you learned from reading this book that you would you like to pass on to others?

____

____

____

____

Paraphrasing the ancient wisdom of Rabbi Hillel, "If not you, then who? If not this battle, then what battle? If not now, then when?" At some point in our lives, we all must decide what we will stand for. Without vision, we will not live the life we were meant to live.

MOMS and families who are willing to fight for their children must stand together in this battle to make a true difference. Joining in this effort can change the outcome emotionally, psychologically, socially, financially, and legally. Over the centuries, it is through women that change has often taken place, and this battle is no different. Join MOMS as we transform the lives of our children who in turn will change life as it is for future generations:

- POWER to face the unknown
- PASSION to endure the tragedy
- PREVENTION to stop further harm
- PROTECTION for MOMS and children

PERSEVERANCE TO STOP
THE GENERATIONAL CYCLE OF MOLESTATION.

As a young woman, I did needlepoint. If I looked at the back side of the needlepoint, it was an absolute mess. It had knots and hanging strings, made no sense, and showed no sign of accomplishment. However, as I worked, I began to see a picture develop on the front side. When I finished, the needlepoint picture was gorgeous. At times we look at one perspective, and we forget there is a bigger picture. It is imperative that MOMS keep the long-term picture in mind as they fight the small, everyday battles.

Even more, as we see the bigger picture, we must remember that other MOMS exist; we are not the only ones fighting this battle. Perpetrators want to keep MOMS isolated and needy, but they do not have to win this battle.

It is time for us to join one another and speak as ONE for our hurting children. We have an opportunity to make a difference by telling everyone MOMS will NOT quit, but will continue fighting by applying all we have learned about ourselves, our children, and the perpetrators to make a difference in the world of child sexual abuse. How can you make a difference in the life of a child in need of protection? Please contact me and share your story. YOU can make a difference in this battle of child sexual abuse.

Listed below are resources that may further help you in your journey to protect children.

RESOURCES

Allender, Dan B. *Wounded Heart: Hope for Adult Victims of Childhood Sexual Abuse*. 1990. Colorado Springs, CO: NavPress, 2008.

Beattie, Melody. *Codependent No More: How to Stop Controlling Others and Start Caring for Yourself*. Center City, MN: Hazelden, 1986.

Braswell, Linda. *Quest for Respect: A Healing Guide for Survivors of Rape*. Tucson, AZ: Pathfinder Publishing, 1996.

Cloud, Henry and John Townsend. *Boundaries: When to Say YES, How to Say NO, to Take Control of Your Life*. Grand Rapids, MI: Zondervan, 1992.

Cowman, Mrs. Charles E. *Streams in the Desert: 366 Daily Devotional Readings*. 1928. Grand Rapids, MI: 1965.

Eldredge, John and Stasi Eldredge. *Captivating: Unveiling the Mystery of a Woman's Soul*. Nashville, TN: Thomas Nelson, 2005.

Frankel, Estelle. Sacred Therapy: *Jewish Spiritual Teachings on Emotional Healing and Inner Wholeness*. Boston, MA: Shambhala, 2005.

Gunaratana, Bhante. *Mindfulness in Plain English*. 20th anniversary ed. Somerville, MA: Wisdom Publications: 2011.

Hazelden Meditation Series. *Each Day a New Beginning: Daily Meditations for Women*. New York: HarperOne, 1991.

Hemfelt, Robert, Frank Minirth, and Paul Meier. *Love is a Choice: Recovery for Codependent Relationships*. Nashville, TN: Thomas Nelson, 1989.

Johnson, Toni Cavanagh. *Helping Children with Sexual Behavior Problems: A Guidebook for Professionals and Caregivers*. 4th ed. 2011. Available at www.tcavjohn.com

Kearney, Timothy R. *Caring for Sexually Abused Children: A Handbook for Families & Churches*. Downers Grove, IL: Inter Varsity Press, 2001.

Levine, Peter and Ann Frederick. *Waking the Tiger; Healing Trauma*. Berkeley, CA: North Atlantic Books, 1997.

Lew, Mike. *Victims No Longer: The Classic Guide for Men Recovering from Childhood Sexual Abuse*. New York: HarperCollins, 2004.

Louden, Jennifer. *Woman's Comfort Book: A Self-Nurturing Guide for Restoring Balance in Your Life*. New York: HarperCollins, 1992.

McKinnon, Marjorie. *Repair for Kids: A Program for Recovery from Incest and Childhood Sexual Abuse*. Ann Arbor, MI: Loving Healing Press, 2008.

McKinnon, Marjorie. *Repair for Toddlers: A Children's Program for Recovery from Incest and Childhood Sexual Abuse*. Ann Arbor, MI: Loving Healing Press, 2011.

McKinnon, Marjorie. *Repair Your Life: A Program for Recovery from Incest and Childhood Sexual Abuse*. Ann Arbor, MI: Loving Healing Press, 2008.

Nelsen, Jane. *Positive Parenting*. 1981. New York: Ballantine Books, 2006.

Peck, Scott M. People of the Lie: *The Hope for Healing Human Evil*. 1983. New York: Touchstone, 1998.

Pelzer, David J. *A Child Called "It": One Child's Courage to Survive*. Deerfield Beach, FL: Health Communications, 2005.

Rothschild, Babette. *The Body Remembers: The Psychophysiology of Trauma and Trauma Treatment*. New York: W.W. Norton, 2000.

Shapiro, Francine and Margot Silk Forrest. *EMDR: Eye Movement Desensitization & Reprocessing, The Breakthrough "Eye Movement" Therapy for Overcoming Anxiety, Stress, and Trauma*. New York: HarperCollins, 1997.

Sinor, Barbara. *Gifts from the Child Within: Self-Discovery and Self-Recovery through Re-Creation Therapy*. 1993. Ann Arbor, MI: Loving Healing Press, 2008.

Warren, Rick. *The Purpose-Driven Life*. Grand Rapids, MI: Zonderzan, 2002.

Wilson, Barbara. *The Invisible Bond: How to Break Free from Your Sexual Past*. Colorado Springs, CO: Multnomah Publishers, 2009.

Wilson, Barbara. *Kiss Me Again: Restoring Lost Intimacy in Marriage*. Colorado Springs, CO: Multnomah Publishers, 2009.

Young, Wm. Paul. *The Shack*. Newbury Park, CA: Windblown Media, 2007.

WEB

Lamplighter Movement. *The Lamplighters*. 2008-2012. www.thelamplighters.org

Male Survivor: Overcoming Sexual Victimization of Boys & Men. 2007. www.malesurvivor.org

RAINN. *Rape, Abuse & Incest National Network*. 2009. www.rainn.org

Stop It Now! 2008-2012. www.stopitnow.org

Survivors Network of Those Abused by Priests. www.snapnetwork.org

REFERENCES

Below are some research sources supporting the information in this book.

Berliner, L., & Elliott, D.M. (2002). Sexual abuse of children. In J. E. B. Myers, L. Berliner, J. Briere, C. T. Hendrix, T. Reid, & C. Jenny (Eds.), *The APSAC handbook on child maltreatment* (2nd ed., pp. 55–78). Newbury Park, CA: Sage Publications.

Bolen, R.M. (2001). *Child sexual abuse: Its scope and our failure.* New York: Kluwer Academic/Plenum Publishers.

Briere, J.N. & Elliott, D.M. (1994). Immediate and longterm impacts of child sexual abuse. *The Future of Children, 4,* 54-69.

Briere, J.N. & Elliott, D.M. (2003). Prevalence and psychological sequelae of self-reported childhood physical and sexual abuse in a general population sample of men and women. *Child Abuse and Neglect, 27,* 1205-1222.

Baumrind, D. (1968). Effects of authoritarian parental control on child behavior. *Child Development, 37,* 887-907.

Childhelp. (2012). National child abuse statistics. Retrieved from http://www.childhelp.org/pages/statistics

Cyr, M., Wright, J., Toupin, J., et al. (2002). Predictors of maternal support: The point of view of adolescent victims of sexual abuse and their mothers. *Journal of Child Sexual Abuse, 12(1),* 39-65.

Daigneault, I., Hébert, M., & Tourigny, M. (2004). Personal and interpersonal characteristics related to resilient developmental pathways of sexually abused adolescents. *Child and Adolescent Clinics of North America, 16(2),* 415-434.

Douglas, A.R. (2000). Reported anxieties concerning intimate parenting in women sexually abused as children. *Child Abuse & Neglect, 24,* 425-434.

EMDR Institute. (2011). Research overview. Retrieved from http://www.emdr.com/general-information/research-overview.html

Finkelhor, D. (1994). Current information on the scope and nature of child sexual abuse. *The Future of Children, 4,* 31–53.

Finkelhor, D., Cross, T., & Cantor, E. (2005). How the justice system responds to juvenile victims: A comprehensive model. *Juvenile Justice Bulletin, NCJ210951.* (CV62B)

Finkelhor, D., Ormrod, R., Turner, H., & Hamby, S.L. (2005). The victimization of children and youth: A comprehensive, national survey. *Child Maltreatment, 10,* 5-25.

Gilgun, J.F. (1995). We shared something special: The moral discourse of incest perpetrators. *Journal of Marriage and the Family, 57,* 265-281.

Gilgun, J.F. (1994). Avengers, conquerors, playmates, and lovers: A continuum of roles played by perpetrators of child sexual abuse. *Families in Society, 75,* 467-480.

Gilgun, J.F. (1988). Self-centeredness and the adult male perpetrator of child sexual abuse. *Contemporary Family Therapy, 10,* 216-234.

Gilgun, J.F. (1988). Why children don't tell: Fear of separation and loss and the disclosure of child sexual abuse. *New Designs in Youth Development, 8,* 16-20.

Gilgun, J.F. & Gordon, S. (1985). Sex education and the prevention of child sexual abuse. *Journal of Sex Education and Therapy, 11,* 46-52.

London, K., Bruck, M., Ceci, S.J., & Shuman, D.W. (2005). Disclosure of child sexual abuse: What does the research tell us about the ways that children tell? *Psychology, Public Policy, and Law, 11,* 194-226.

Mendel, M. P. (1995). *The male survivor: The impact of sexual abuse.* Thousand Oaks, CA: Sage.

Minnesota Center against Violence and Abuse. (1995- 2012). *MINCAVA Electronic Clearinghouse.* Retrieved from www.mincava.umn.edu

Putnam, F.W. (2003). Ten-year research update review: Child sexual abuse. *Journal of the American Academy of Child and Adolescent Psychiatry, 42(3),* 269-278.

Snyder, H.N. (2000). Sexual assault of young children as reported to law enforcement: Victim, incident, and offender characteristics. United States Department of Justice. Retrieved from http://bjs.ojp.usdoj.gov/content/pub/pdf/saycrle.pdf

ABOUT THE AUTHOR

Kim Johnson, a licensed clinical social worker, has worked in the mental health field since 1990 in the Sacramento, California area. She has a Master's of Social Work from San Diego University and specializes in Children, Youth, and Families. She has also earned a Pupil Services Credential, which allows her to provide counseling services in school settings. She has been employed both in the public and private sector, inpatient and outpatient settings, and has assisted people ranging from ages two to eighty-three. Kim has helped clients to overcome past trauma and conflicts, alter dysfunctional patterns, and actualize their potentials toward recovery and fulfillment.

One of Kim's areas of specialization is trauma or Post-Traumatic Stress Disorder (PTSD), and she utilizes EMDR (Eye Movement Desensitization & Reprocessing) to treat this disorder in approximately 80 percent of her private practice patients. She has earned special certification through the Eye Movement Desensitization & Reprocessing International Association (EMDRIA) to treat PTSD. She also teaches EMDR Therapy.

Kim's other specialties include play therapy for children; art therapy for children and adults; depression; anxiety disorders; marital/family issues; survivors of physical, emotional, psychological, and/or sexual abuse; stress management; and bereavement and loss.

Kim's primary goal and passion is to assist children, teenagers, and adults (male and female) by joining each one on his or her journey to understanding, change, healing, and transformation.

Kim Johnson is available for speaking, consulting, and other engagements.

Book Orders

This book is available at volume discounts; please contact Kim Johnson for more information.

Speaking Engagements

Kim Johnson is a well-respected and successful international speaker who can share real-life inspirational stories of healing for your audience and provide valuable, up-to-date information while customizing her message to meet your conference or meeting's theme. Her memorable presentation will challenge your audience to pursue and accomplish more for the wounded at heart, specifically Mothers of Molestation Survivors. When you need a speaker for your next event, contact Kim Johnson.

Consulting

Kim is available for consulting regarding therapy needs for a particular case or to help an organization implement therapy programs.